New White Sandals

A Memoir

Toula Siakotos

Library of Congress Control Number: 2012907159
ISBN: 978-0-6156-2624-6
ebook ISBN: 978-1-63001-754-5

This book was printed in the United States of America.

www.newwhitesandals.com

ACKNOWLEDGEMENT

I like to thank my son, Nick, for his suggestions,
wise counsel, and editing.

To Nick & Erica

Nicky, Lucy & Ben

CONTENTS

Prologue

A little girl dressed in black and wearing new white sandals, a small dot among hundreds of people stood alone on the crowded upper deck of an ocean liner. She looked to be around ten or eleven years old, was just under five feet tall and weighing maybe sixty-five pounds. The wavy blonde hair framing her olive-complected face was parted on the left and held back with bobby pins. She was tiny, skinny. Looking at her, one would think she was a refugee escaping to a distant land in the hope of a brighter future. She looked out at the vast ocean through bewildered blue eyes.

As she looked about sadly, she took in the sight of her fellow travelers: men, women and children of all ages, a mix of personalities and moods. She saw chatting young men and women huddled together in intimate circles, their laughter was in stark contrast to the somber mood around them. Others set stoically, holding fast to overstuffed bags. Middle aged men and women came sharply into focus as they grabbed hold of the deck railing. Wiping away tears, they waved their final goodbyes to loved ones on shore. About to embark on a life-changing journey across the Atlantic, many on board made the sign of the cross, their lips moving in silent prayer to God for a safe trip.

Anxious young men comforted their weeping wives by holding them close; together, as if in a kind of trance, they rocked to and fro to ease their sorrow. Oblivious to their circumstances, happy children scampered across the deck, their mothers haplessly chasing after them.

What the little girl noticed most of all, however, was that the people around her were making the long voyage as families, which made her acutely aware that she was traveling by herself—alone—at the tender age of eleven. Traveling without her family at such a young age was terribly painful for the girl. Indeed, it was a pain that would outlast the trip to America itself and linger deep within her for years to come.

Circumstances had forced her out of the family nest, as it were, too soon. Holding back bitter tears, she reminded herself that there were, in fact, people on board that she knew.

There was Eleni, a beautiful, spirited young woman in her early twenties—a fellow villager—who had left Greece for America some six years earlier. She was returning to America after having visited her family. Having crossed the Atlantic Ocean once before, she appeared to be handling her second trip quite well. Along with her uncle Panagiotis, who also served as her sponsor, and young cousin Basilis, Eleni was returning to her home in Chicago.

Eleni was wearing a short beige skirt and a sleeveless white blouse. Her thick, glossy, black hair bounced with life when she walked. Her dark, almond shaped eyes and olive-skinned face were consonant with what is considered the facial features of a modern-day Greek.

Panagiotis, her middle-aged uncle on her mother's side, was an unassuming man. Short, balding and chubby, the fifty-five year old had cinched his dark slacks around his round belly. The sleeves of his wrinkled white shirt were folded at the elbow. His bushy brown eyebrows stuck out behind his oversized black sunglasses. The owner of a successful textile business, Panagiotis was well-off. He was a widower, having lost his wife to ovarian cancer several years earlier.

Ten year old Basilis was a miniature copy of his father. Like his dad, he was an easy-going young fellow, who had yet to shed his baby fat. He wore beige shorts, a white, short-sleeved cotton pullover, and brand new leather sandals. His dark hair was cropped very short. Like his father, he wore dark rimmed sunglasses, but his fit better. Father and son were playful with one another. Panagiotis was quite attentive to Basili, putting his arm around his shoulder, mussing his hair affectionately, and generally having fun with him. Basilis, in turn, giggled a lot, and seemed very content, if not a little spoiled.

Oh, where was my baba to hold me close and protect me? I asked myself, wiping away a tear.

Although it comforted me to have traveling companions, I didn't know them all that well, and this reinforced my sense of isolation. I wanted to be back home with my family with every fiber of my being.

"Toula, Toula, there you are," Eleni called out to me. With a broad smile and sparkling eyes, her feet hardly touching the deck, Eleni rushed toward me. Her full red lips matched the rouge on her high cheek bones. Big, gold hoop earrings caught the sun's rays, while the gold bangles on her left wrist jingled as she walked. A gold crucifix hung on her chest.

I was captivated by Eleni. She was extremely outgoing and upbeat, quite different from the way I felt. Instead of listening to what Eleni was saying, I stared at her fast moving lips, not really comprehending what she was saying.

"Toula, Toula, aren't you hot in that black dress?" Eleni asked. Even though it was summer, I was dressed in black, still mourning my father who had been murdered two-and-a-half years ago.

It was June, 1952, and we were on our way to America. My mind was burdened with thoughts of my family, home, and the village where I was born and spent the first eleven years of my life.

Toula was a common nickname. My given name was Demetra. I was named after my maternal grandfather. I was Georgia and Adonis Siakotos' youngest child. I had three older brothers. My sister Effie was the eldest child of all, fifteen years my senior. Being the first-born son, Niko enjoyed certain privileges. Yianni and Konstantine—Gus for short—were my other brothers. We were all born three years apart.

We were each nursed for about two years. My mother, like other women in the village, believed that breast-feeding served as a kind of birth control. I had overheard my mother and neighboring women discuss this miraculous discovery many times. They regulated the birth of their children and limited the size of their families in this manner, or so they thought.

"Make sure you breastfeed your last one for at least two years," the women would say.

"I wish I could stop mine at two," I remember Eugenia, one of the neighbors, say. "The other day, my four year old climbed on my lap, undid the buttons to my blouse and was ready to suck on my breast; I had to scold and push him off my lap. Imagine!"

"I know what you mean, they never seem to get enough," responded her friend Petroula. The women sitting around a circle by now to have their occasional chit-chat and indulge in a little gossip, laughed and nodded their heads knowingly.

I had also overheard, on more than one occasion, that my parents were not exactly thrilled in having me. They already had four children whom they could barely support. Worse yet, I was a girl. Not only in my small village, but throughout Greece girls were considered second-class citizens—liabilities, really. Now my parents had the additional worry of saving enough money for a dowry sufficient in size for me to marry into a decent family. This would be a hard if not impossible task since money was always scarce. And that was not all! Girls represented the added risk of dishonor should they turned out to be *bad girls*. I soon found out that *bad girls* were those who simply associated with boys. This meant they were loose, indecent and immoral, which reflected poorly on the family. Like other parents in town, my parents feared that their daughters might have sex before marriage which was absolutely the worst thing a girl could do to her family. And, God forbid, should we get pregnant; we'd never marry after such a disgrace. Until our dying days we'd be remembered as those *bad girls* who had a baby out-of-wedlock. We would become outcasts, living out the rest of our days in shame.

I had heard of this worst-case scenario enough times that my whole mission in life was to be a *good girl.* I did not associate with boys at all and discouraged all attention from the opposite sex. I was totally consumed with being a *good girl.*

There was yet another reason that my birth was not welcomed. My mother felt humiliated that at the age of forty-two she was still having sex with her husband and I was proof of that! A woman's sexual behavior, married or not, played an important part as to how a female was viewed by both the community and her own family. Sex, it seemed, was for procreation and fulfilling the husband's physical needs, and, of course, that was a wife's duty. Perish the thought that the woman herself should enjoy sex. No, that would be immoral and sinful.

I tried modeling myself after my big sister Effie. Try as I might, however, I just couldn't identify with her. We were so different. She was so pretty for one thing. She had thick, lustrous hair, brown eyes, and much taller than I could ever hope to be. Plus, she was the easygoing type. She didn't seem to fear being branded a bad girl. She wasn't very vigilant about keeping her distance from boys. She seemed comfortable around men. She just went with the flow, as it were, and didn't seem to struggle with emotional hang-ups, like I did.

My parents related to her as an adult, often seeking her advice. I wanted to be acknowledged too, but I was too young and could not be taken seriously. I was constantly dismissed by pretty much everyone in my family. I don't know how many times I heard the same refrain: "You are too young. You don't understand. How could you possibly know?" Even when I insisted on being heard, my parents and siblings alike would typically respond by saying, "Please, don't insist. Be quiet," shooing me away. My parents preferred Effie to me, which necessarily affected my self-esteem. I felt sad and angry, which manifested in daily headaches and stomachaches.

Skopi

I was born in a small village called Skopi, a hamlet of approximately five-hundred homes built on a hillside three-hundred-fifty feet above sea level. It is situated on the outskirts of Tripoli, a merchant city of about twenty-thousand people. Located one-hundred-twenty miles southwest of Athens, Tripoli is in the center of Peloponnesus, a transportation hub for both trains and buses. Skopi sits between the ancient cities of Sparta and Olympia. Because of its inland location and high altitude, the summers are hot and dry, and the winters cold. The terrain is rocky with scattered trees and brush. It is surrounded by wooded mountains, the tallest and closest of which is Mount Mainalon to the northwest.

Most of the houses two stories high and scattered across the hillside, were made of stucco. They had courtyards, and were topped with red tile roofs. Narrow, winding streets meandered from the town square throughout the village.

As grandparents played an important role in Greek culture of the day, a typical family consisted of three generations all living under the same roof. Adult children were morally obligated to take care of their elder parents. In turn, grandparents made themselves useful by helping around the house and caring for the children.

A small grocery store and coffee house stood in the town square. Most of the local men would gather there daily. They'd banter back and forth, passionately arguing the issues of the day. They drank demitasse size cups of *metreo,* thick, Turkish coffee, while counting, again and again, the bright colored beads on their *komboloe,* which is to say, their worry beads. During their quiet moments, they indulged in *kollitsina,* a favored card game, similar to gin rummy.

The square also served as a terminal of sorts, where the occasional visitor, arriving by taxi or bus, would be received. This was always something of an event. Locals would rush to the square to see who was visiting their village.

"Who is it, who is it?" they would ask one another. "Could it be `*o brouklis?*"—a term describing a former member of the village who had immigrated to America years before, and had now returned in a shiny new car, wearing a brand new suit, and unquestionably, lots of cash in his pockets.

The square also served as a staging area for celebrations of religious holidays of which were many, and important historical events such as Greece's independence from Turkey on March 25, 1821. We would eat, drink, dance and come together as one on those occasions.

The community well, from which the women folk would fetch water, was located on the outskirts of town. Filled with crystal clear and delicious water, the barrels were strapped to donkeys and mules and carried home for drinking, cooking, bathing, laundry, and for general household cleaning. Incredibly, there was always enough water for everyone no matter the time of year.

The town's grammar school, a red-tiled, two-room schoolhouse was just a short walk from home. First, second and third grades were taught in one room, while fourth, fifth and six grades were taught in the adjacent room. The teachers came from out of town, usually from Tripoli.

The church, a beautiful edifice made of white stucco walls and a bronze dome, was just a few meters from the schoolhouse. The cemetery surrounded the church. The priest, Father Manolis, executed a variety of religious duties, from Sunday liturgies, to presiding over births, weddings, deaths, and numerous religious holidays throughout the year. People went to him for the required confessions before holy communion and for any other matter of the soul. He would even make house calls in order to rid homes of evil spirits the tenants claimed dwelled within. Most everyone in town was religious and attended services pretty much every Sunday.

Built by my maternal grandparents in the late 1800's, our home sat on a crest and enjoyed a panoramic view. It had an enclosed courtyard made of whitewashed stone. Storage rooms on one side of the courtyard were filled with the year's harvest: potatoes, wheat, corn, garlic, onions, figs, walnuts, almonds, olives, and all types of fruit, both fresh and dried. A separate, relatively dark room, with cold, concrete walls housed a huge barrel filled with my father's homemade wine.

A long staircase from the courtyard led to the house. The kitchen had a fireplace for the dual purposes of cooking and heating. There was a utility room where Mother made bread and kept flour and other non-perishable foods.

I shared a small bedroom with my brothers, Gus and Yianni. My parents and Effie had bedrooms of their own. The large, airy living room opened onto a long terrace. A grape vine stretched over the arbor covering the entire terrace; it had been planted by my father when he and my mother were newlyweds. It consistently produced large, sweet white grapes, which hung tantalizingly through the lattice. In summer, we'd spend most of our time on the terrace, eating, visiting, relaxing, and enjoying the view. We often gathered there to eat our main midday meal. The table would be covered with various food and drink, including cheese, olives and bread—made by my mother—my father's homemade wine, and, occasionally milk from our goats or sheep.

Dessert would invariably be the plump, white grapes hanging from the arbor few feet above the table. We would simply reach up at the succulent grapes, and then drop them directly into our mouths. I still remember how fun that was, and how sweet, and fragrant the grapes were.

When the nights in summer were temperate, my brothers and I would sleep on the terrace. We would drag our bedding outside and entertain one another with stories. Yianni would tell jokes that seemed to go on forever. We'd fall asleep laughing under a star-encrusted night sky. I sure loved those times!

Family discussions usually revolved around one of the following topics: what was going on in town, how much this or that cost, or, occasionally, politics, both local and national.

"Fish was quite expensive in the open market in Tripoli this past Saturday. I was only able to purchase couple of pounds of cod, but will make do," my mother would say. "Did you hear, Katerina Stavropoulou had another abortion. She's always afraid of having another girl."

"Stavros—you know, a couple of houses down—just bought a handsome-looking cow. He'll sure have plenty of milk for his ever-expanding brood," Father mentioned.

"I heard from our neighbor Katsevou, that the *andartes*—mountain guerrillas—came in the middle of the night last night and took your goddaughter Xrisoula, by force. She's just a couple of years younger than our Niko, around sixteen or seventeen! Poor thing, we have to check with her family," Mother said.

Father shook his head in bewilderment. Confused and scared, I wished they would elaborate, but that was all they said.

Family discussions almost always included, as well, how everyone in the family was responsible for doing his or her part in keeping the household afloat, as it were. We were made to understand that it was a team effort. Everyone had a job, that is, except for me. And I wanted a job, so I could feel that I too was an important part of the family, contributing like everyone else. But I was always told the same thing, "You are too young, be patient, your time will come." I never liked hearing that.

My father would routinely ask my brothers and sister if they had done their chores, and they'd usually respond in the affirmative except, at times, for Yianni, who for some reason or other didn't get around to doing his work. Known to have a short fuse, Father would very clearly express his disapproval. One could practically see the steam coming from his nostrils as he stood up from the table and reprimanded my brother, who by now, had hung his head in shame and fear.

"Yianni, what is the matter with you?"

While attempting to control his anger, he looked directly at my brother and thundered.

"This is not the first time you have failed to meet your obligations to this family! I want you to get up right this minute and do what you should have done a week ago already!"

Yianni did what he was told, but my father's outburst had left us all shaken. Although I felt sorry for my brother, I was also frustrated that he had provoked Father's anger and that it now enveloped us all.

I'd watch Mother bake bread and cook using the domed earth oven my father had built in the back of the house. She fueled the oven with wood and coal. Placing her hands a few inches above the hot coals, she knew exactly when the oven had reached the right temperature. She would then place the baking pans inside and close the aluminum door with dried animal dung she'd softened with water. I could hardly wait for the food to be ready. The aroma wafting from the oven generated such an appetite in me. Sprinkled with fresh oregano, sweet basil, rosemary, thyme, garlic, lemon juice, salt and pepper, the food—crisp on the outside, tender in the inside—always tasted delicious. Although we never had it often enough to suit me, my personal favorite was lamb and potatoes.

Mother and Effie also baked lots of different sweets, especially *koulourakia, a* doughnut shaped butter cookie served at Easter, the most important religious holiday in the Greek Orthodox faith. Here too, only after much pleading was I allowed to help out. Mother would let me pour milk into the batter or crack the eggs. If I was really lucky, they would even let me roll and shape some of the cookies; that was always lot of fun. I closely watched their technique, and did my best to copy Mother's and Effie's style, afraid that if I didn't do a good job, they'd decide that I was still too young and should not participate. I was meticulous, shaping the cookies just like they did. My mother would monitor my progress by saying, "No, that is too thin, or too thick, too small, or too big," but mostly, though, she'd be encouraging, "That's about right, Toulaki."

Father had quite the reputation as a winemaker. It was not unusual for locals to come by the house—ostensibly for a visit; but what they were really after, according to my mother, was a taste of my father's wine. Mother nonetheless made sure to set the table with bread, cheese, olives and, of course, some of Father's wine for our guests. While generally pleasant with visitors, Mother had no trouble telling them to come back another day when they had overstayed their welcome. Occasionally guests might ask for another glass of wine, but my mother had rules, and she had no qualms enforcing them.

"*Ela, file, alli mera.*" Another day, my friend, she'd say, as she gently nudged them toward the front door.

Produce buyers from Tripoli and environs would visit our farms to buy grapes, potatoes, wheat, prunes and olives. My father had to negotiate hard for the best price. He would point out how big and unblemished the potatoes were, how large and sweet the grapes. "You can eat these sweet grapes, or make wine, or both. You can't find better grapes anywhere— they are the best!" He'd pick up a handful of olives, large and black, ready to be cured for the table or pressed for rich, virgin olive oil. He'd hand out samples of his fresh and perfectly formed prunes. "They are wonderful for your health. Here, please, taste how sweet they are."

I knew that this must have been difficult for my father, for he was not a born salesman. But he was very proud of his crop. He would end up getting a good price with buyers coming back season after season. We lived off the proceeds from these sales, reinvesting what was left in upkeep and cultivation of the land. Most of the families in town farmed and lived off the land as well.

My mother's brother was killed in WWI. Her lone remaining sibling, a sister, had taken a small portion of the family land as a dowry when she married several years earlier. The rest of the land and family home were left to my mother. When my father married my mother and moved into her home, he also brought his own land to the new union. Combining their parcels, my parents were known in the village for their sizable real estate holdings. It proved, however, to be a huge responsibility for such a young couple, my father being just eighteen and my mother twenty-four at the time of their marriage. Needing help, they began hiring migrant workers willing to work hard for a reasonable salary, three squares meals a day, and all the wine they could drink.

Manoula

I sometimes called my mother *manoula*—mommy in Greek. I'd refer to her as *manoula* either when I felt especially close to her or when I felt ill and needed her love and attention.

I viewed my mother as a strong, independent and self-sufficient woman. She was maternal, compassionate and protective of her family.

I thought I had the best mom in town. She was sweet, kind, loving, which is not to say that she couldn't be firm when need be. Although she had a very busy life, she always had time for us. As much as I admired her judgment, I truly respected my mother's loving approach to parenting.

Although she was sociable, involved in her community and had many friends, she could still be mistrustful of others. Even so, when she had the time, she enjoyed chatting with her neighbors. When she felt especially happy, I could even detect a slight sense of humor creep into her conversation. She'd let her hair down, as it were, sometimes even to the point of playfulness.

There was another side to my mother, however, and that was of a woman in perpetual mourning. She dressed in black from head to toe every single day. As was the custom in Greece in those days—especially in villages—women remained in mourning for family that had passed on— even if their passing had transpired years before.

One could still see, however—despite the black *mantili*—a delicate face of fine lines, high cheekbones, and large, deep-set brown eyes. Having parted down the middle, she would braid her long, wavy, chestnut-colored hair and pin it into a bun. She was a very pretty, slightly built woman with a subtle sensuality.

It made me sad to see my mother always dressed in black. I often fantasized seeing her in short, colorful dresses. I so much wanted to see her truly happy, and free of the constrains of custom. I'm sure my siblings felt the same.

One day my brother Gus and I came up with what we thought was a brilliant idea; we'd all pitch in and buy our mother a dress of a different color.

"What do you think of the idea?" we asked our brothers and sister.

"What color should the dress be then?" asked Effie.

"Navy blue is about as far as we could go. She'd reject any other color as inappropriate," she quickly offered, answering her own question. At least it is a beginning, I thought.

We scrounged up what money we could and gave Gus the job of going into town and buying the dress. It took him no time at all to find the perfect, little navy blue dress in a small family-owned store in Tripoli.

I felt both excited and nervous when Gus brought the dress home. What if Mother didn't like it? What if she refused to wear it? What if the very idea of not wearing black so offended her that she became angry with us? I decided it would be best not to entertain such thoughts.

We all gathered in the living room to present the dress to our mother. As usual, our father wasn't home.

"Manoula, come. Come join us in the living room," we called out to her.

"What is it? What's wrong? What happened?"

"No, no, everything's fine. Sit down. Please." I moved a worn wooden chair in front of her.

Now that we had her full attention, Gus walked into the room holding the dress wrapped in newspaper behind his back. Glancing at us first, he then rested his eyes on our mother. He brought the dress from behind his back with a certain pomp. All eyes were fixed on Mother as Gus let the newspaper wrapping fall to the floor, revealing the brand new navy blue dress.

Mother looked at the dress and said, *ti einai auto,* what is this? It was so quiet, you could have heard a pin drop. We all started pleading with her, "It is your new dress from all of us—p-l-e-a-s-e, p-l-e-a-s-e—try it on, it is yours to wear. Please, *manoula,* say you'll try it on!"

Standing up, she looked at the dress, took a step backward, looked away, then looked at the dress again. Laughing nervously, she said, "I can't wear this dress, it's not black," reminding us—as if we didn't know—"I am in mourning, remember?"

"At least you can try it on," we pleaded.

She looked at us sadly, knowing how disappointed we'd all be if she didn't try the dress on. Poor *manoula,* what was she to do? Hew to tradition and remain in black, or make her children—and perhaps even herself—happy?

She dwelled on this question for a few seconds, then suddenly grabbed the dress from Gus' hands and disappeared into the next room. Waiting anxiously for her to reappear, I tugged on Gus' shirt sleeve so hard, I nearly tore a hole in it. We looked at one another in great anticipation when all of a sudden she walked into the living room wearing—what else—the navy blue dress!

"So, are you happy now?" she asked, slightly annoyed.

We didn't even bother to answer, just stared at her in a mixture of awe and disbelief. By simply putting on that dress, my mother's face and figure was that of a much younger woman. Her new dress was much shorter than her usual black—just a couple of inches below the knee, revealing her shapely legs, which, by the way, we'd never seen before. Her new dress was made of soft cotton, and had a thin belt. Small navy blue buttons ran between the rounded collar and the waist. For the very first time I saw Mother's small waist and delicate frame. She looked terrific!

We were all so pleased! I was so excited that I jumped up from my chair and started dancing round and round, clapping my hands, till I felt dizzy and fell to the floor. We all laughed in utter joy. We asked our newly made-over, startlingly pretty mother to turn around, so that we could see how she looked from the back.

"That wouldn't be necessary," she snapped. Then seeing how important it was to us, she complied.

The dress fit like the proverbial glove. I set there thinking, if only she could throw away her black *mantili*, black hose and shoes—her entire black ensemble—she'd look terrific *every day of the week*. But, I knew that would be asking too much. Standing there in her brand new dress, I thought Mother looked shy, a little embarrassed; who knows, perhaps she even felt guilty that she was not dressed as if she'd just come home from a funeral.

My mother had suffered many losses early in life. She had grown up without her father. Like others in the village, grandfather had emigrated to America when Mother was but a little girl.

"I believe he settled in New York," she'd tell us. "He was a manual laborer, laid railroad tracks. I don't remember much about him, but I do remember feeling different from other kids because my father wasn't home with us. Folks treated me like an orphan, and, to be honest, I felt like one. I felt embarrassed, different from the other kids in the village. Feeling different, kept me from making friends, I guess, even though I was well-liked. The loneliness, the isolation gnawed at me. The next thing I knew, he was dead, having been killed at work somewhere in New York."

No other information of the accident was given.

"My mother—your grandmother—was devastated." Sadness and

shame at his loss passed from mother to daughter. "We all dressed in black and cried pretty much every day. As if that wasn't depressing enough, my mother would also sing the *mirologia*—mournful songs of death—several times a day.

We struggled financially after your grandfather's death; he'd always sent us money from America. We had to adjust to our already tight budget. There was very little money for extras. Life at home during this time was pretty rough."

Mother had also lost her beloved brother in World War I.

"Stelios was tall and very handsome. He had black hair and brown eyes. He was athletic and played sports, soccer, mainly. He was also kind. Reliable too. After Father's death, he became the head of the household at the tender age of seventeen. He took good care of us. I was proud of him. And I loved him very much."

It sounded to me that Mother felt about her brother the way I felt about my own brother Gus. I understood how painful it must have been for her—and her mother and sister—to lose him, especially at such a young age.

"He wanted to become a doctor and had entered medical school when he was drafted into the army. He served in a medical unit and was killed while aiding a wounded soldier on the battlefield.

I remember my mother screaming when she learned of Stelio's death, pulling at her hair, running out into the street, anguished over the loss of her only son. And, I'll never forget that very day when my mother changed into a black dress, sat in a chair facing the living room window, and began to rock back and forth, in kind of trance, singing the *mirologia*.

My sister Basiliki and I took charge of the household after that; we hired a crew to work the land. We worried about our mother all the while as she sank into an ever-deepening depression. She seemed to be waiting for death to come and end her misery.

Basiliki and I would often join her in singing the *mirologia*—usually after dinner—for we too grieved the loss of our brother." Three women in black trying very hard to survive during an extremely painful time. "We felt terribly alone—and vulnerable, too—not having a man around the house," she trailed off.

The windows shut, desiccated flowers in pots on the window sills, a place that looked and smelled of death. Neighbors tried to help out and offer comfort to the trio of women in black, but it was all in vain.

My grandmother, sadly, transformed from a strong, dynamic woman—very much involved in her community—into a woman who wanted nothing more than to vanish from the face of the earth. Losing both husband and son was just too painful for her to bear.

Life was so stressful for my mother that she too became depressed. A few years later, when my mother was around twenty, relief for my grandmother finally came in the form of death.

"Your grandmother died from a broken heart," Mother claimed. "She joined her husband and son in the afterlife." Within a couple of years of my grandmother's death, Mother's sister married and moved to her husband's village, about twenty-five miles away. Alone in the family home, Mother tried for a while to manage things alone until my father came along.

My Father the Socialist

F ather came from a large family, nine children in all. He was the sixth child born to my grandparents, Argiro and Triantafilos Siakotos. His father and three elder brothers had emigrated to America when my father was a very young boy. My grandfather eventually returned to his family in Greece while his sons remained in America.

My father was of medium height, around five feet eight inches tall. His thick, shortly-cropped brown hair framed an oval face. He had blue eyes—a rare trait among modern Greeks—and an olive complexion. He also had a square, little mustache reminiscent of Adolph Hitler's. I remember feeling funny about that since I knew what an evil man Hitler was.

My father was a serious, hardworking and responsible man. Unlike my mother, he wasn't very social and kept mostly to himself. He spoke very little, seemingly preoccupied with his own thoughts.

Most days, he'd throw a heavy pea coat over his shoulders and walk alone to work on our land. He interacted very little with us kids and probably not much more with Mother. A very young man burdened with an array of responsibilities, and I wondered how he managed. Sometimes I wondered if he might not be living in a world of his own making, divorced from the real world.

Never once did I see my parents express affection for one another. Never saw them kiss, and only on rare occasions did they share the same bed. More often than not Mother would sleep with us kids, and I always wondered why. Still, I loved it when she snuggled into bed with us. I would sleep closest to her, snuggled up against her, kissing her, hoping she would return the affection. And she often did, but never for long. I got the distinct feeling Mother felt there was something wrong with physical affection—even with her own kids.

Like most people back then, my parents expressed their love by taking good care of us, or as best as they knew how. They wanted us to be good children, to pray and to attend church, not that that any of these expectations were ever forced upon us. They wanted all of us—but especially my three brothers—to be good students, so they encouraged them to pursue higher education. For their daughters, they wanted nothing more than good husbands. We did our best to fulfill our parents wishes as this was our way of returning their love and constancy.

I found both of my parents, but especially my mother—as I understood my father hardly at all—to be rather progressive thinkers, despite their limited education. I saw this in their lack of judgment of others; their willingness to cooperate and be friendly with their neighbors and fellow villagers. They were inclusive, shared with others what little they had. They were compassionate, empathetic. They were pragmatic, reliable people. One could count on them. And, they handled jealousy and gossip, common with some locals, as best as they could, and didn't engage in this kind of pettiness themselves. We felt ourselves lucky having caring parents who wanted only the best for us. None of us was ever spanked, our mother's reproving look sufficient discipline to kept us all in line.

Much to my surprise, Father, in his own quiet, solitary way, decided to run for mayor of Skopi. I was equally surprised of his election to a two-year term! His political foes often railed against him for being a socialist. On account of his politics, many in the village neither liked or trusted him; in some quarters, he was even detested. But, my father never felt he had to explain or justify his political beliefs. Of course, I was just plain confused not knowing what exactly a socialist was. Didn't matter to me anyway; I was pretty proud of him.

At that time Greece was struggling to recover from the civil war that had followed WWII. Incredible atrocities had occurred throughout Greece. Many people died as a result of civil strife—some even in our own village. *The andartes*—the communist guerrillas holed up in the mountains—were responsible for some of the worst atrocities. There was a feeling among some of his political opponents that my father was indirectly responsible for those deaths.

For his part, my father kept pretty much to himself, typically trying to avoid conflict whenever possible. I suppose it's fair to say he was his own man, quiet and steady. I could never really tell how he felt, because, here again, he communicated so very little. It was actually kind of comical how little my father talked. To my eyes, he looked alone and sad pretty much most of the time. Even so, my parents felt successful as a couple for they found meaning and success through their children. They had raised good kids. Knowing how important this was to them, we did our best to please our parents—that is, with the notable exception of my brother Yianni.

I treasure a memory of my father from the time I was six years old. I awoke early one morning to find him still in bed. Now, as one might imagine, this was really quite unusual. I was pleased as punch, however, to have my father home in the morning. While Mother was busy making breakfast, I nervously tiptoed to his bed, and slipped in next to him, hoping that this would not annoy him. With his head straight up, staring at the ceiling, he now slightly moved his head so as to touch mine. He then slowly lifted his left arm and wrapped it around my shoulder, gently nudging me closer to him. Finally, he planted a tender kiss on my right temple. How I loved the feel of his fatherly embrace and those few precious moments I spent with my normally elusive father. If I think back, I can still feel those same warm and loving sensations. To the best of my recollection, this was the one and only time my father expressed his love for me.

Gus

C losest to me in age, my brother Gus was my role model. As the others were too busy to watch after me, the job fell to Gus by default. We were a lot alike—or so I liked to imagine—since I loved and admired him very much. At my young age, I was completely unaware of one *major* difference between us, however; he was a boy, and so had privileges I didn't have. He could be himself and did pretty much what he wanted. He would go out with friends and stay out late and not hear a word of disapproval from my parents. He'd rendezvous with girls, and that seemed okay too. He'd up and disappear for long periods of time, and that didn't appear to be a problem either.

When I tried to exercise my own freedom, I was summarily reprimanded. When I objected, I was informed that, being a girl—and a young one at that—I simply couldn't follow my brother's lead.

"You are a girl. People will talk. They'll say you come from a bad family. Anyway, you are much too young, you need to stay home."

The admonition to behave confused and upset me. I felt ashamed, believing that I was behaving inappropriately, and that made me a *bad* girl. While Gus never had to worry about being a good kid, I worried all the time that I *was* a bad kid.

Like me, Gus was slightly built. Unlike me, however, he had fine, wavy brown hair and big brown eyes. While I resembled Father, he looked like our mother. A brilliant student, he was the head of his class in both elementary and high school. Ever available, classmates would come to him for tutoring so they could pass their comprehensive exams. He taught youngsters how to ride their bikes, and his friends how to win at card games. He was often picked first for school sports, and despite his small stature, performed extremely well. He was given first choice of roles in school plays. Even the village priest would often ask my brother to read a passage from the Bible at Sunday service. Old people in the village would sometimes seek out his advice, as well. He was generous with his time no matter his own responsibilities.

Girls adored him too. I had often seen girls flirt with him. They didn't seem to have the same "curse" that I did—that they would be perceived as being *bad*. He had girlfriends, and I think he had sex with them too. It was not uncommon for the girls' brothers and fathers to bang on our heavy courtyard door demanding to see my brother, threatening to "beat the shit out of him." My mother always protected her youngest son by lying, "He isn't here, now go away."

As much as he liked the girls, Gus was a responsible, loving, and compassionate member of the household. He'd often bring me my favorite candy and gum—and maybe even the occasional trinket—when he came home from high school in Tripoli. He'd be equally thoughtful where Mother was concerned. He'd bring groceries home—and even cooked once in a while—surprising everyone when they came home exhausted from the fields.

When I cried or when I was sad, he'd place his arm around me and ask, "What's the matter, Toulaki? Don't you feel well?" He'd take the time to listen and to comfort me. When I needed to go to the outhouse in the middle of the night, he'd go with me, knowing I was too afraid to go alone.

I remember how he'd join me in prayer every night. We'd kneel side by side, our hands clasped under the religious icons of Saint Nickolas—our patron saint—the Virgin Mary and Jesus. In accordance with orthodox custom, the icons hung in the living room on the wall facing east, illuminated by the *kanteli,* a small olive-oil vigil light. This was a sacred and special time for me, and I felt grateful that my brother was there too, kneeling and praying beside me. I have to admit, though, that I was never quite sure if Gus was genuinely religious or just prayed for my sake.

I have especially warm memories of one summer's evening as we were making our way home. It was a hot, humid, middle of the summer night. The air was filled with the sounds of nature: grasshoppers rubbing their legs together, birds chirping sweetly, horse's hooves hitting the ground. The night sky was clear and filled with what seemed like a million stars. The full moon was out that night too, lighting our way. I could swear that the moon at one point looked like as if it was smiling at us.

I couldn't take my eyes off the jolly moon while walking alongside my brother. I soon became convinced that the moon was following us; this both mystified and frightened me. I kept quiet about this for quite some time, but finally I asked my brother.

"Gus, I think the moon is following us."

Gus looked up at the moon, then down at me, and started to laugh. I liked the sound of his sweet, mischievous, laughter; I instantly felt relaxed. He put his arm around my shoulder and proceeded to demystify the moon for me.

"The moon looks like it's following us because it is huge and is so far away. No matter how fast we walk, Toulaki, we wouldn't be able to outrun it." We actually tried outrunning it for a stretch, but the moon kept pace.

"We can't pass its reflection either," Gus continued, "It moves right along with us."

Taking his time, he spoke in a manner appropriate to my age. I remembered how special I felt, not only to have his attention, but that my brother had enough confidence in me to bother explaining the mystery of the moon's seeming omnipresence at all.

"You see, Toulaki, the moon isn't following us at all. It just seems that way."

"Oh," I said rather in awe. Nuzzling closer to him, he kept his arm around my shoulder a little while longer.

On another occasion, he spoke—seemingly to himself—of life and death and our purpose on earth. I recalled his thoughtful explanation, but mostly . . .

"I believe that there is something greater than us, something bigger than the obvious. Perhaps there *is* a God."

Although Gus may not have been exactly religious, he was quite obviously of a spiritual bent. Who knows, perhaps his life was even guided by spiritual principles.

I found my brother quite complex; there was so much about him I didn't understand. In some ways, he was inaccessible, mysterious. I believe others in town felt the same way about him. Perhaps it was his particular spirituality, or his unique way of looking at life that eluded us all.

He sometimes seemed nervous. His hands would shake slightly when he ate. He must have been suffering from some kind of emotional stress, the cause of which, of course, I can only guess. Perhaps he was doing too much, being pulled in too many directions. Perhaps he found the weight of the world, of living, overwhelming, intolerable. He might have felt responsible for us all—for our spiritual, psychological health—in that my father was neither physically nor emotionally available.

During the summer, he'd become physically ill. Though never definitively diagnosed, we all figured it was hay fever. We could only treat the symptoms: the headaches, the runny nose, the blood shot eyes, the agitation, and general listlessness. We would wait patiently until fall when the symptoms abated, only to return the following summer. We worried and prayed for him.

Everyone in our family loved and admired Gus. I thought of him as the heart and soul of our family. He was loved and respected in the community, as well.

I got a kick out of watching him mount a horse. While the horse galloped just a few feet ahead of him, he'd quickly place both hands on the horse's rump and jump on its back from behind. Seeing this, all the kids in the neighborhood would beg Gus to teach them how they too could jump on the horse and ride the way he did.

"Please, Gus, please show us how you do it."

"Ok, ok, I will show you."

And he would indeed show them, in a fun kind of way, over and over again, until they got the hang of it

Another of his tricks was using Mother's large, wooden flour sifter to catch birds. He did this by holding the flour sifter upright with a thin but sturdy stick. He'd tie a string to the sifter at the other end to which he'd hold on. He'd sprinkle bread crumbs on the ground under the sifter. When the birds swooped down to peck at the crumbs, he'd tug on the string, causing the string to collapse, thus entrapping the birds. He was fun, ingenious, intense, loving, and dependable; a really well rounded person despite his youth.

It confused me, made me angry that every time I tried to imitate him, my mother and sister in particular, would come down on me like a ton of bricks. Baffled, they'd shake their heads and say, "She's different. We're going to have trouble with her." Naturally, I took this to mean that I was indeed a *bad girl*. Feeling judged and rejected by my mother and sister, I redoubled my efforts at being a good girl.

It never quite sunk in, however, that I was suppose to act different than my brother. Gus was my role model like it or not. Whether conscious or not, the decision to model myself after my brother exposed me to a great deal of reproach not only in childhood but throughout my life for that matter.

Yianni

A handsome, blond, blue eyed young man, resembling the actor, Paul Newman, Yianni was a unique—strange even—character. He was creative, musically inclined and a born comedian. He was not interested in manual labor, avoiding it whenever possible. This really upset my father. Mother didn't much like it, either. The rest of us resented him for his idleness, because it meant that we had to do his work as well as our own.

Yianni enjoyed passing his time entertaining us—and the hired help—with his unique brand of humor. He was a natural comedian, and even though everyone resented him for not buckling down and carrying his own weight, we all laughed till we cried when Yianni was on one of his signature rolls. Comedy was his métier and not physical labor. He was happiest making people laugh.

My brother also aspired to be a professional musician, to lead his own band, and to play at various celebrations in and around the village; this was how he envisioned earning a living. He bought a used violin and taught himself to play, paying for lessons when he could afford to. He even sang a little.

Unfortunately for Yianni, Mother and Father did not encourage pursuit of his dream. They saw Yianni as being lazy, a dreamer, and figured he wouldn't amount to much. The condemnation he routinely received from family and village folk alike had a profoundly negative affect on my sensitive brother. In time, he grew to doubt himself, withdrawing inward. He dropped out of school, otherwise did very little, and gradually began to exhibit bizarre behavior. He began to develop fears, near phobias. Despite still being basically a kid, he began to suffer from hypochondria.

He played cruel jokes on friends, and even young children. On hot summer days, he'd get the little kids in the neighborhood drunk on wine, and then would tell them to climb onto the hot tin roofs of nearby houses. The kids would try to do what he told them, over and over again in fact, but in vain. Sliding down the hot roof burning themselves, they would end up in tears. At that point, he'd tell them they could stop. He'd give them a few coins for trying. He'd laugh, for he found it quite amusing.

Another of his mean spirited tricks was a fairly common prank that he played on Taki, a friend of his. At our vineyard, several miles away from the main home, we had a second home where my family and the hired help would use during the year, especially at planting and harvest time. There was another vineyard near by, and a running creek with fairly deep water that ran for miles. Taki spent many a night there, just as Yianni did at our vineyard. My brother knew full well that Taki was the nervous type. Indeed, his anxiety might have even exceeded my brother's.

Taki was afraid of the dark. He believed in ghosts and feared that they would come in the dead of night and hurt him. Yianni took cruel advantage of this superstition. He and his friends donned white bed sheets, floated into Taki's vineyard and home on a starless night, and scared the bejesus out of poor Taki! They ran in crazy circles around Taki's house banging on pots and pans over and over again. They climbed onto the roof of the house and oohed and aahed hauntingly. They continued this till an absolutely terrorized Taki could bear it no longer and ran out the front door screaming bloody murder!

"Leave me alone! Leave me alone!" He'd head for the creek to drown himself for he was driven close to madness. Only with Taki at the literal and figurative edge—about to swan dive into the creek in his undies—did Yianni bring the practical joke to an end. They removed the white sheets, and let the sticks, pots and pans fall to the ground. Yianni then grabbed Taki by the shoulders and said, "All is well my friend. There are no ghosts, we were just having a bit of fun."

By now, of course, poor Taki had practically crawled out of his skin. Taki developed such fear of my brother that he did his best to avoid him no matter the time of day.

"You stay away from me, Yianni Siakotos, I beg you."

Needless to say, my brother developed quite a reputation in town as a practical joker. Some kept their distance from him, while others rather unaccountably enjoyed his uncanny sense of humor.

Yianni continued to play the violin with some success. He began playing with a loosely formed band at weddings, baptisms and other events. Unfortunately, however, my parents still didn't approve of his line of work, and so my brother continued to suffer emotionally. He became increasingly introverted. Without the needed support, Yianni gave up his dream of becoming a professional musician. Eventually, he joined the army. He served in the military police, stationed in Salonika in Northern Greece.

I had a soft spot for my brother, and tried to make up as best as I could to what I thought was unfair treatment by my parents. I'd laugh at his jokes, supported his dreams, but it didn't really help. By now, his spirit broken, Yianni had changed. He buried his true talents, and turned into a different person. It made me sad to see him abandon his true self.

The Nazis

"It is just not possible for you to remember Second World War let alone Nazis occupying Greece and living in our home," Mother would often tell me. She was sure I was mistaken, that I couldn't possibly remember such things for I was just a baby when it all happened.

It was early fall. The weather was beginning to change. There was a chill in the air. Folks were finishing up in the fields for the year and were getting their homes ready for the long, cold winter ahead. Throughout the year, families across Skopi had stockpiled enough food and provisions to last the winter. They had stored rice, potatoes, flour, a variety of beans, and both fresh and dried fruit. Cooked meat packed in lard was stored in large ceramic jars. The wine barrel was full. Folks made sure they had enough firewood and enough feed for the livestock. They repaired the windows and doors to their homes. Heavy, hand woven wool blankets were brought out from storage trunks. Folks wished one another a comfortable, restful, winter, knowing that they would not see one another much until spring thaw. The tranquility engendered by this annual ritual was shattered by rumor that had spread like wild fire.

"The Germans have entered Greece, and they are headed our way!"

From tranquility to chaos, people were terrified and helpless now! They vacillated between the following two thoughts: We will die at the hands of the Nazis just as our predecessors did when the Turks occupied our town and country; or, everything will be okay, this too will pass.

Repressed fear and hatred residing in the Greek psyche of the four-hundred year occupation of Greece by the Ottoman Empire resurfaced. Hundreds of thousands of Greek men, women and children perished—many burned alive inside locked Greek Orthodox churches—throughout an occupation that lasted from the fifteenth century to 1821, the year Greece won its independence. The generations that followed independence were weaned to fear and hate our Turkish tormentors. These terrible memories now came flooding back with a vengeance.

The village was buzzing: "The Nazis had arrived! Their war machine had reached our humble, little village. Their tanks were in the town square. Everyone hide."

People scattered like frightened animals. The square and streets were abandoned as folks holed up in their homes. Mothers drew their children close, disappearing behind locked windows and doors. Folks clung desperately to one another, hoping that they might be overlooked if only they disappeared into the dark recesses of their homes.

Although she did her best to keep her composure, I could see from the look in my mother's eyes that she was terrified. "No one is to leave this house. Understood? Now everyone inside!" she commanded, her voice dark and disturbed. She too shut the doors and windows. Like others in town, we didn't light our kerosene lamps. We just sat in darkness, waiting and praying to God to save us.

But, before we had time to think—or do anything else for that matter—the Germans were upon us. They were looking to find commodious accommodations before nightfall. They marched through the village, banging on doors and storming inside homes, pushing the occupants aside. Suddenly we heard the heavy footfalls of their jackboots outside of our front door. And before we knew it, six soldiers were inside our courtyard, rushing up the stairs invading our home. They hurried through the house. In no time, they nodded to one another that our home would do. We were scared to death. We huddled together en masse in a corner. My father was protective of us at first—and dare I say, a little defiant—but he quickly decided that wasn't the best course of action. Better to do as ordered—that is, accommodate our captors.

The Nazis moved in!

They were a frightening sight, what with their distinctive military uniforms, shiny jackboots, bullet belts strapped across their chests, and pistols at their waists. Some of them wore heavy, black overcoats, which made them look even more sinister. They were all fairly tall and trim. Their hair was cropped short. Their narrowly-set, piercingly blue eyes projected a dark sense of impending evil. They appeared disciplined and well organized, seeming at times almost like robots. Their occasional laughter was brief and controlled.

A tall man, around thirty years of age, whose features betrayed a spirit of severity, seemed to be the officer in charge. We never learned his name. He would simply march back and forth, giving orders to his men who were standing at attention.

In time we learned that there were around two-hundred Nazis stationed in town. We also learned that we weren't the only ones in the village who had the unwelcome pleasure of bunking with the Nazis; apparently they had taken possession of several other homes in town.

While we were confined to the kitchen, they occupied the rest of the house. They filled the place with guns and ammo. They had radios and a telephone. They brought in boxes filled with canned meat, sardines, sausages, coffee, sugar, and chocolate bars. We were told that we would need to supplement their food.

"You will give us what we need while we are here. Is that understood?" the chief officer told us in German-accented Greek. Our sense of panic grew as the intimidating tone of his voice increased.

They wanted to know where the lavatory was and where they could get fresh water. They asked for bedding, and eating utensils. They settled in. They stayed pretty much to themselves from then on, but we knew full well that we were at their mercy. Though their Greek was practically non-existent, some of the soldiers spoke French or English. Since both my brothers Nick and Gus spoke a bit of French, the Germans occasionally tried to converse with them, but communication was still quite limited. The language gap only added to our anxiety, since we couldn't even guess what they were thinking, what their plans for us were, how long they planned on occupying our home. We lived from moment to moment.

They had questions for us all the same. They wanted to know who exactly lived in our home—ages and gender. They questioned my father as to his political leanings. The same questions were asked of our fellow villagers. They wanted to know if there were known communists living in the village. Naturally, we said very little in response, afraid of provoking them, or somehow implicating our fellow villagers. Frightened by these interrogations, we nonetheless kept up a front, desperately trying to hold on to some small part of our identities—to exercise some measure of control—as illusory as that might seem now.

Most of the time they just sort of hung around the house—Nazis in repose—reading, tuning into the radio, scribbling on thick, white notebooks, or conversing with one another. There were days when they would have visitors—their fellow Nazis. Sometimes they would get together in the courtyard for brief conversation after which a few of them would leave again. On other occasions they might just pace back and forth.

Once a week Mother was allowed to leave the house in order to do the shopping and run errands. Mother did a pretty good job of keeping her fears in check, remaining calm, and composed. She cooked for them— three square meals a day. She ended up using all of the rice and potatoes we'd stored up for the winter feeding the Germans. As they demanded meat with practically every meal, Mother had to slaughter all our livestock, which consisted of about a dozen chickens and several heads of lamb and goat. They finished off all the eggs, milk and sugar we had and all the dry food we had stored in bins. The Nazis enjoyed Father's wine with their evening meal. Of course, our own food intake left a lot to be desired.

An unexpected thing happened while they lived at our home. They were intrigued by me. They said that with my blond hair and blue eyes, I reminded them of their own children back home in Germany. They would beckon me to come close, trying to entice me with chocolate bars. I loved chocolate, and remembered vividly the few times I was lucky enough to have had this wonderful treat. While glancing at my mother to see what I should do, I timidly approached the soldiers. I knew they expected as much, but I was also hoping for some chocolate. They extended their hands, offering me not one but two chocolate bars; for a second, I thought I had died and gone to heaven. I couldn't believe my luck. They drew me close and smiled sweetly at me. Too intimidated to look at them, I kept my eyes fixed on the floor while gently rubbing the shiny, slippery paper covering the chocolate bars. My innermost desire, however, was to rip off the paper and devour the chocolate as soon as possible. I felt myself salivating, but I had to keep up appearances.

One of the soldiers enjoyed bouncing me on his knee. It felt like I was riding a horse and found myself giggling. They would sometimes toss me in the air and catch me as I came down. They would laugh and I would laugh along with them. They liked having me around. Perhaps, I was a diversion for them, a toy to be played with, a respite from their mission. I was rather frightened of them, but I sure did love those chocolate bars. I noticed, by looking at my mother's eyes, that she felt helpless around the situation. There wasn't much that she could do, other than keep a watchful eye over me.

At night, in hushed voices, we prayed that they would leave our home, and our country as soon as possible. I pleaded with God to come and take them away.

Living with the Nazis was beyond bizarre. We were consumed with fear and guilt. We were afraid that they might kill us. We felt guilty that we were accommodating and—some might even say—fraternizing with the enemy. I imagine that my parents—particularly my father—must have felt impotent; humiliated not being able to defend his family, his home from this intrusion. I would look at my parents, trying to imagine how they felt. Their eyes—to me—looked blank, paralyzed by fear, afraid to move or even think. We were all struggling to cope with this incredible nightmare.

I'd occasionally wonder what our captors thought of us. Were they frightened too? Were they going to kill us? Were they going to massacre everybody and raze the village? How long were they going to stay in Greece?

Then, without warning, some twenty-four days into their stay, they just up and gathered their belongings and left. As they were leaving, the one soldier who had taken a special liking to me, paused and knelt down beside me. Looking at me, he smiled. He then placed his hand gently on my shoulder and handed me a chocolate bar, saying, *"yiasou mikroula"* good bye little one. To our surprise and gratitude, there were no casualties in our town.

The country as a whole, however, was devastated by war and occupation and its economy and infrastructure lay in ruins. Greece suffered more than four-hundred-thousand casualties during the occupation. A vicious civil war followed in 1946 between the British and American-sponsored conservative governments and leftist Greek guerrillas that lasted until 1949.

Andartes

As they were between the ages of eighteen and forty, Father, Effie, and Niko, were subject to involuntary conscription by the *andartes,* communist guerrillas. Whenever there was a rumor of an impending raid—always in the middle of the night—all three would scurry to a hiding place in the back of the house behind the outdoor oven. Father had dug a hole there large enough to accommodate them. It was approximately five and half feet high by five to six feet wide. Once inside, a piece of sheet metal would be placed over the opening. Mother would shovel dirt on top till it wasn't visible. For good measure, she would toss debris and dried leaves on top of the dirt. For air, Father had outfitted the hole with a long, round metal tube that extended beyond the fenced area of the yard. It was difficult, if not impossible, for anyone to find this hiding place. One would need to go under the house, pass through the barn which often smelled of animal excrement, open a heavy wooden door, find their way behind the clay, wood burning oven, and still, there wasn't anything to indicate that there was a hiding place there. It was a very clever idea. My father, sister and brother hid in this place a number of times and were never discovered.

I remember one night in particular when the guerrillas knocked on our front door. The heavy banging woke us. Mother threw back the bed covers and, putting on a dress and sweater, told us in a hushed voice to stay quiet. She calmly walked to the front door. She hardly had a chance to open it, when four soldiers—three men and a woman—stormed into the house. We were all shocked to see Marika standing before us in fatigues, combat boots and a beret and, fully armed! She was the eldest sister of one of my friends. Her family and mine were close friends, not to mention distant relatives. Father was Marika's godfather. She pretended not to know us, and for safety's sake, we played along. This was indeed a shock as Marika was still in high school and had never expressed political views of any kind. In fact, I had seen her on the street, close to her home, it seemed, only about a month earlier. Then I remembered the rumor that she had been abducted by the guerrillas not long before.

She certainly looked and behaved like a guerrilla, demanding money, food and heavy, winter coats.

"Uncle Adonis, Niko and Effie, where are they?" she inquired.

"They are away," said Mother.

"What do you mean, away? Where are they, and don't lie to us!" she bellowed, placing her hand threateningly on a holstered revolver.

"Uncle Adonis is away on business; I'm not sure where. We are in need of an additional horse to work the land. He heard that there was one available for sale somewhere, but, as I said, I don't know where."

Scoffing at Mother's explanation, Marika raised her right arm dismissively.

"And Niko and Effie, where are they?" she asked impatiently.

"They are not here either. I would assume that they are in Tripoli. They occasionally rent a room instead of coming home after school; it all depends on the amount of school work they have."

I was so scared, I trembled. I moved closer to my brother Gus, tugging nervously on his shirt sleeve. He put his arm around me, but looked straight ahead.

Pushing us aside, the guerrillas began searching the house, moving hurriedly from one room to the next. My mother slowly took a few steps toward us. She nudged us all into a corner and whispered, "Be quiet. Stay calm."

The guerrillas hurried down the stone stairs and then made a quick right turn that led under the house, stormed through the barn—spooking our horse and several chickens in the process—and opened the heavy door leading to the back of the house. Mother followed behind. We stayed put in the corner, gripped with fear that this time they might actually find the hiding place. I imagined the guerrillas dragging my father, brother and sister back with them into the mountains, never to be seen nor heard from them again. Fortunately, they had trouble keeping the heavy door open, which gave us hope that they might give up, turn around and leave. While struggling with the door, they quickly scanned the area, and motioned to one another that they didn't believe anyone was there.

"Let's get out of here," barked one of the guerrillas. As they swept past Mother, Marika looked directly at her and said, "We'll be back."

Before leaving, they grabbed whatever they wanted—heavy clothing, pots and pans, food and what little cash we had left. We held on to one another for sometime after they had left, not saying a word. Father, Niko and Effie remained in their hiding place for at least fifteen to twenty minutes, not coming out till they felt certain the coast was clear. We all made the sign of the cross, thanking God that, once again, our loved ones had evaded capture.

I listened to my parents talking to one another afterwards.

Father said, "What happened to Marika could happen to anyone of us. We could be taken away and brainwashed just like that poor girl."

"We must remain vigilant," said Mother. "We must not reveal the hiding place to anyone. You can't trust anyone these days."

They nodded in agreement. Mother repeatedly made the sign of the cross, and whispered thank you to almighty God.

Murder

I was nine years old sitting at my desk in fourth grade when I heard that my father had been murdered.

Mr. Paraskevopoulos, a middle-aged, and rather serious man was the school-master responsible for the operation of the school. He also taught the combined fourth, fifth and sixth grades. Miss Petropoulou, a very pretty woman in her twenties with shoulder length shiny dark brown hair who wore make up and smelled of perfume taught first, second and third grades. She also taught music; I especially enjoyed singing the popular songs of the day. There was also Mr. Petrakos, our part time teacher who taught theology and substituted for Mr. Paraskevopoulos and Miss Petropoulou. We attended elementary school for six years, then graduated to high school in Tripoli for an additional six years.

The school week was five-and-half days; we studied the Bible for a half day on Saturdays. Students would take turns reading the Bible during Sunday liturgy.

School days began with an hour of exercise in the schoolyard which consisted mainly of calisthenics. We then had a light breakfast of warm milk and bread. After breakfast came hygiene. Our hair, our small faces, our little hands, even our ears were thoroughly examined. If the headmaster was not happy with what he saw, he would register his disapproval by striking the tops of our hands with his wooden ruler. I was so afraid of this happening to me, I made sure to give myself a sponge bath before going to school each morning.

We wore school uniforms: short, pleated navy blue skirts and white blouses for the girls, navy blue shorts and white shirts for the boys. We carried our books and school supplies in leather bags that hung across our shoulders.

The lessons were difficult. Classroom instruction was equally challenging. The teachers would pace back and forth, clutching the dreaded ruler. They would pose questions, and we knew what would happen if we didn't have the correct answers—the ruler would come down on our hands pretty hard. Miss Petropoulou, to her credit, would never strike us. Unannounced exams were a frequent occurrence. Moreover, students could not be promoted to the next grade unless they passed a comprehensive exam. And, of course, there was plenty of homework.

On this particular summer day, as in each day of the school year, we recessed briefly upon the arrival of the postman; he would usually arrive around noon. Students would take the mail home to their parents at the end of the school day. Just about every family had a child in school. Those who didn't, would walk to school for their mail upon hearing the postman's bugle.

"*Herete*" the postman greeted the teacher. He would then commence a roll call.

"Petrakos," "Here."

"Spiliotopoulos," "Here."

"Sideris," "Here."

"Panagiotopoulos," "Here."

He continued till all the students had come forward and picked up their mail. An older man, whose children were now adults and living in America, walked into the classroom.

"*Kalemera*," good morning, he quietly greeted the schoolmaster and postman.

Instead of taking his mail and then his leave, as was his habit, this time he lingered, talking nervously with the school master. The students, now feeling restless, focused their attention on the whispered exchange between the two. An absolute stillness settled in the room. The students leaned forward in their chairs, craning their necks to make out what exactly was being related in such hushed tones.

"There was a murder in town, it just happened." "What?" responded Mr. Paraskevopoulos with alarm.

"What are you saying?"

"A murder in our town? What?" repeated the schoolmaster.

Mr. Paraskevopoulos couldn't believe his ears. He cupped his hand over his mouth and shook his head in utter disbelief. He leaned toward the man, certain that he had not heard him correctly.

"I am afraid Adonis Siakotos was killed," the man explained. He paused, shock registering in the teacher's eyes.

"His son Niko was also shot, a bullet to the left temple. Fortunately, I believe the boy has survived. He was taken by ambulance to the hospital."

Dumbfounded, Mr. Paraskevopoulos turned to face his students. This was unheard of; never before had he known of a murder in Greece, let alone in our small village. He looked at us all. Then, his bewildered eyes rested on me.

I looked away. I couldn't bear to meet his gaze. A chill came over me as I struggled to make sense of the words I had just heard. My head was spinning, my senses failing, something inside me had instantly, drastically changed.

"Did I hear right?" I asked myself. "Did he say Adonis Siakotos and Niko? But, it can't be! He can't be talking about my father and brother!"

I was too afraid, too traumatized to ask what had happened. I tried blocking out the intolerable truth that my father was killed and my brother gravely wounded.

I was afraid I might faint and fall to the floor. I knew only one thing—I wanted to disappear! I slumped into my desk chair and felt as though I were slipping into the abyss. Despite not wanting to hear or feel anything, I heard the schoolmaster's voice.

Addressing me formally, he said, "Demetra, you are excused, please go home."

The sound of his voice triggered so many emotions: anger, fear, humiliation, shock, sadness—but above all, horror that such a terrible thing had befallen my family and me.

I didn't want anyone to look at me, but I could feel all eyes in the room were on me. I did not want anyone's pity. Try as I might to lift my head—to look up—it felt as though it weighed a ton. I couldn't lift my gaze from the black hole that seemed to have opened in the floor. All I wanted was to distance myself from the combined stares of my classmates, teacher, the postman, and the visitor who had delivered the tragic news. Time seemed to have stopped. Shock and dismay suffused the classroom.

Conscious of the teacher's gaze all the while, I forced myself to stand up and then march, like a wooden soldier in a Nutcracker play, out of the classroom. I marched out the front door, down the stairs, and finally out into the street. Reluctantly, I raised my head and gazed fearfully up the hill in the direction of my home. Though I had walked this hill countless times before, on this occasion it felt like climbing Mount Olympus; I was afraid I wouldn't be able to manage it. I was totally drained of energy. I felt like one of the hunched-back old woman one would see trudging through the village. I could already hear the village folk whispering.

"That crazy old man Kalimanis, killed Adonis Siakotos. Ah, he had it coming."

I could see, or so I imagined people gathering, whispering, difficult to fathom that such tragedy could possibility have happened in this quiet, little village. I'm not sure how I got up that hill as I couldn't feel my legs under me. As I approached the village square, men and women, as in a Greek tragedy, were all in a frenzied state—whispering, crying, embracing one another. They averted their eyes as I passed. It almost seemed I could hear them thinking, *the poor little girl, now an orphan.*

Would I make it home as the schoolmaster said, "Go home and see what happened?" Would I disappear as I so much wanted; perhaps I should run away. I speculated on the scene that awaited me at home. As I neared my house, increasing numbers of people were moving in the very same direction. It seemed as if every single person in the village was now walking toward our house. *It really must be true,* I thought. *It really has happened.* I felt lost among the throng, all lamenting the murder of a fellow villager.

"*Po, po, po, ti egine edo?* What has happened to us, to our village, to poor Adoni? What is going to become of his family, his poor children? I shudder to think."

I finally made it home. The large wooden door leading to the courtyard, usually shut, was now wide open, jammed with people. My heart was racing.

As I continued walking ever so slowly, then entering the courtyard, I thought I saw something so horrific, I could hardly breathe. I reluctantly pushed through the crowd and moved toward my mother and sister who were bending over my father's body on the ground.

Oh, my God, is it true? I looked for any signs of life—I desperately wanted my father to be alive. As tears began to roll down my cheeks, I placed my hand over my mouth to muffle the primal scream that seemed about to escape my lips.

Forcing myself to take a closer look, I saw that my father's body was stretched out on top of the entrance door to the house which had been taken off its hinges and placed on the ground. Parts of his white shirt and dark pants were soaked in blood. There was a large pool of blood under him. I cringed watching my mother and sister clean the blood off him, tears staining their faces. They gently washed the crimson blood off his face and arms with small white clothes; they did this, over and over again.

"Please stand back. Give them room," someone pleaded.

The villagers murmured among themselves. People crossed themselves. Others asked God to forgive Father of his sins. With trembling hands, women wiped away tears while covering their mouths with black handkerchiefs. I tried to keep my balance, as the ground was shifting beneath my feet.

I noticed my sister had already changed into a black dress, one of my mother's. *No, no, it simply can't be,* the voice inside of me persisted. Finally, I forced myself to confront what I fought so hard to deny—my father was dead, the words pounding in my head. I felt like a knife had slit my heart wide open. I found it hard to breath. I needed to get away. I looked frantically, desperate for my brothers, Gus and Yianni, *where are they, where are they?* They were nowhere to be found. They had accompanied my wounded brother Niko to the hospital, I later learned.

My blank eyes gradually moved toward my mother, *how painful this must be for her,* I thought. I felt terrible grief for her, remembering all the people that she had already lost. I wanted to go to her, to tug on the edge of her black apron to let her know that I was there with her. Instead, I walked past her—and my father's body—and continued zombie-like up the stairs into the house. I walked into the living room and then out onto the terrace, where I crumbled onto the warm concrete floor. I leaned against the wall, my limp legs curled under me.

I felt very much alone, numb and tragically sad. In all of the commotion, no one seemed to have noticed me! I needed someone to comfort me. To my great relief and gratitude, I felt the warm, wet, scratchy tongue of my little puppy Hasan. Over and over, he licked my face, arms and hands.

Hasan was our eight-week-old German Shepherd puppy. He was gray with white markings on his belly and a small white spot on the left side of his snout. He was fat, playful and very lovable. I looked at my little puppy and gently picked him up and held him tightly to my chest. It calmed me to feel his little heart beating next to mine. I kissed my puppy and he continued to lick me. I was thankful for this little bundle of fur, and wondered if he sensed my great sorrow.

Hasan and the Gypsies

E very summer gypsies would come to town. I'm not sure where they came from. Locals said they came from the Middle East, Montenegro, Serbia, and other parts of Eastern Europe. They all seemed to belong to the same clan. I'd guess there were probably about a hundred of them spread over ten families.

They entered our town, men on horseback, women and children in wagons followed behind. Dressed in bright colored clothing of reds, oranges and yellows, they whooped and hollered making their arrival known—to the locals' consternation.

The women tended to be tall and slim. They wore their black hair long. They had dark lined, almond shaped eyes and an olive complexion. Their lips were painted a deep red, and their cheeks sparkled with red rouge. Some of the women pinned their hair up—mostly on one side—where one could see large gold or silver hoops dangling from their ears. They wore lots of bracelets—ten to twenty on each arm—and long necklaces hung down their chests. Their colorful dresses and skirts were ankle length, one side usually pulled up and tucked at the waist. They fancied ruffled, sleeveless blouses with plunging necklines, all the better to reveal their often ample décolletage. They quite literally jingled when they walked; their body decorations gave rise to musical sounds. They looked exotic, sexy, provocative, and somewhat sinister.

The men typified the descriptor tall, dark and handsome. Partial to lightweight clothing that helped them weather the summer heat, some men also sported small earrings, bracelets, and gold chains. Like the women, they exuded sex appeal and mystery.

The children too wore colorful clothing, but their clothes were often soiled and torn in places. They looked unkempt with dirty faces and hair. They would hold on to their mother's skirts, crying oftentimes, and looking quite sad. Their mothers would either ignore their cries altogether, or try to muffle them by openly breastfeeding them.

Our visitors, or should I say intruders, rode in on brightly colored blankets strewn on their horses as they galloped into town. The caravans also included mules, donkeys and a number of dogs. They carried their belongings—bedding, clothing, pots and pans—openly in their wagons. They were a sight to see, believe you me. For us kids, it was like watching the circus come to town. They camped all summer long in a large grassy clearing about the size of a baseball diamond at the foot of the village.

The town folk didn't like having the gypsies in their midst. They found their presence intrusive, and resented them. They resented their drinking, their carousing, their use of hashish. They kept the town awake what with their violin and clarinet playing, and banging on their drums late into the night. They sang, danced and generally created havoc.

Folks in town thought the gypsies lazy and immoral; they looked upon them as degenerates, sexual libertines whose children were born out of wedlock. They did not seem to have a religion either—their lifestyle was one without principles. Moreover, they begged for their survival.

Just about every day they'd infiltrate the town, banging on doors for food and money. Once denied, they would threaten folks with curses and spells. Since Skopi's residents were mostly a superstitious bunch, they often complied, not wanting to rile the interlopers up. Although I too was afraid that they might cast a spell on me and my family, I nonetheless found myself drawn to these strange people. I found them attractive, mysterious and free-spirited.

One day, before leaving for a day's shopping in Tripoli, Mother told Gus and me to lock the door and not let anyone into the house, least of all the gypsies. Of course, we assured her that we wouldn't . . .

Gus was reading a magazine and I was playing marbles on the floor when we heard a knock at the door; it must have been late morning. We looked at one another. Recalling what our mother had told us, we didn't open the door. The knocking persisted. We could tell, of course, from the sounds of wailing children and a language we didn't understand, that gypsies were at the door. As the banging continued, out of a combined sense of fear and curiosity, Gus and I decided in the end to open the door ever so slightly and take a look. Bad move. The second we opened the door, an arm covered in bangles reached in. The hand connected to this arm moved rapidly in front of our faces like a slithering snake; this was accompanied by a voice begging for food and money.

In Greek, a woman's voice pleaded, "My children are hungry! They need milk!

Please help us! *Puhlease!*"

"We don't have anything to give you. Now go away." Another bad move.

It didn't matter what Gus said; the woman just kept begging. While one of her brood clung to her dress crying, she breastfed the other. I felt sorry for them. I urged my brother to give them something. He stood his ground, however, telling the woman again to beat it. The gypsy woman grew furious in response.

"You had better help us or I am going to put a curse on your family that will last a lifetime."

Scared out of my wits that she might actually put a curse on us, I pleaded with my brother to give her something. "Please, Gus, give her something, anything, just so they'll go away and leave us alone! Please!"

A rather large bag—orange, yellow and green in color—hung from her right shoulder. Matching tassels hung along the bottom of the bag and around the strap. I noticed that something was moving inside. This beautiful—and now fully exercised—gypsy reached into her bag and—lo and behold—pulled out a little puppy! I could only see its furry head and front paws. The gypsy offered it in exchange for food and money. I stared into the dark, loving eyes of the little gray pup.

Only six months before, Giseppe, a dog we'd had since before my birth, had died. There had been an outbreak of rabies in town. In order to rid the town of the virus, the sheriff came to our home, and as he had done with other dogs in town, fed our pooch a piece of meat laced with poison. With great sadness, I recalled now how old Giseppe, having eaten the tainted meat, walked away from our house and climbed a hill where he found a spot and waited to die alone. I desperately wanted to be with my dog in his last moments, but my mother would not allow it; she was afraid that our dog might indeed have rabies and could bite me.

So, I watched my sweet Giseppe from our balcony. I prayed that my old dog would die without too much pain. With tears streaming down my cheeks, I waved and blew kisses at my beloved dog as he lay dying.

Although I still missed Giseppe, I really wanted this adorable little pup.

"Can we please have him, Gus? He's so sweet. Oh, Please!"

Gus looked at me with great annoyance then firmly said, "Be quiet, Toula, I'll handle this."

The gypsy kept begging, kept threatening. I could see that Gus was growing afraid of her; he looked worried, less assured. He seemed not to know what to do.

"What if she is telling the truth? And puts a curse on our family?" he asked apprehensively. Finally, reluctantly, he gave in, saying, "We do have a couple of extra eggs. I suppose we could give you those."

"But, that is not enough," she responded aggressively. I see you have plenty of chickens." She looked at the pecking chickens in the courtyard.

"How about a couple of chickens, as well?"

Gus, now very frustrated and angry, feeling pushed into a corner, grudgingly marched off and soon came back holding two live chickens by their hind legs. Their beaks pointing to the ground their wings flailing, he handed the chickens over to the greedy gypsy along with a half-dozen fresh eggs.

The deal was done. The gypsy—and her two little nippers—walked off without as much as a thank you—indeed we could hear her mumbling what probably were curses under her breath as she departed. But, I got my little doggy. We recalled that the gypsy woman had said that she had brought the little puppy all the way from the Middle East. So, we decided to call him Hasan.

As happy as we were to have a new dog in the house, we really worried about Mother's reaction when she found out. After all, we'd broken her rule about not opening the door to strangers. And, we were taken advantage. What were we going to do now? What were we going to tell her? The truth, or we should just make something up? Gus and I didn't say a word. We'd wait until she got home, then we'd face the music, we decided. For now, I was enraptured with my beautiful *Hasan*. To this day, I could still hear my mother's voice, *"you gave them two whole chickens, for this little puppy? You gave them two whole chickens . . . ."*

"Toulaki, Toulaki, where's my little girl," my mother's almost hysterical voice awakened me. I was still holding Hasan, when she scooped me up and wrapped me in her apron, hugging me tightly, not wanting to lose yet another person whom she loved. She walked into a dark corner in the kitchen while I held on to Hasan. She slumped into a chair and began singing the *mirologia,* as her mother did years before when she lost her son Stelios. I hugged her tightly, squeezing Hasan between us. Finally, all the tears that I had been holding back began to seep out. Mother sang the *mirologia,* while I sobbed. Back now from the hospital, Gus and Yianni— and sister Effie too—surround us.

We were startled by the pealing of the church bells conveying to the villagers, *there was a death in our town;* it was now acknowledged by all— our father, at the age of forty-two, was indeed no longer with us.

The Wake

Night fell as we prepared the house for what would be a three day-long wake. Accompanied by two of my aunts, Mother and Effie began the difficult task of cleaning and dressing my father's remains. They began by gently wiping his face and hands with a damp white cloth. They combed his hair—making sure to part it on the left—as he usually wore it. They brushed his mustache. Then they dressed him in a black suit—the only one he owned—and white shirt. They cleaned and buffed his black shoes.

With the help of my cousins, my uncles George and Strati carried my father's corpse into the living room and laid his body on a long table, which was draped with a white cloth. They gently straightened his head, and made sure his hands were properly clasped and placed just below his chest.

The women placed icons of St. Nickolas, Saint Anthony, Christ and the Virgin Mary next to Father's head; still more icons were placed in specific areas of the living room, which now served as a memorial chapel. Chairs were arranged around Father's corpse in anticipation of the procession of mourners that would visit over the next three days. Along with some of Mother's relatives from out of town, it was expected that just about everybody in Skopi would come to pay their respects. Candles that had been placed about the room illuminated the space. Two standing candles—tied with black ribbon—were placed on each side of Father's body. The smell of burning incense permeated the room. Effie closed the windows and shutters, while my brothers hung a large cross, draped in black cloth, on the front door.

As night approached, the house, now quiet and dark, was in mourning. Most everyone—that is, with the exception of relatives, and out of town guests—was gone; this provided us a brief but welcome respite. I fell asleep on the kitchen floor by the fireplace. Someone had placed a blanket over me.

Meanwhile, the family gathered in the living room to discuss both the wake and funeral arrangements. Assisted by Uncle George, who had by now assumed the role of head of the household, Mother wanted to make sure that everything be handled properly. It was a given that all women, including extended relatives would wear black. The men to dress in black trousers and white shirts, and a dark jacket, if one was available. And, a black armband on their left sleeve, signifying the death of family.

I woke to the sound of the *mirologia;* the three-day vigil had begun. Wondering how long I had slept, I rose and walked quietly toward the living room. A group of black-clad women were seated around my father's body. Mrs. Theodorakis, a neighbor and one of my mother's closest friends, was lamenting my father's passing in song. She was soon joined by other women, in a kind of chant.

"You were a good, kind man, and we will miss you."

With heads bowed, they all nodded in accord—wiping away tears— and crossing themselves. They took turns lamenting his loss in singsong fashion.

"Why did you leave us so early?"

"What will your poor children do now?"

"What will become of your poor wife now that you are gone?"

Still, others looked up toward the heavens, pleading with God to "forgive the forgiven of his sins, and welcome him into heaven." They crossed themselves yet again.

They blew their noses loudly and wiped away the tears with large black handkerchiefs. With my mother and sister joining in, this ritual would last till late into the night only to begin again the next day.

Mourners began streaming in at daybreak. They offered their condolences upon arrival. *Zoe se sas, zoe se sas,* life to you, life to you, they greeted family members. They brought vegetarian casseroles, fruit, cheese, bread, and wine; guests would help themselves to the food throughout the day.

Hair covered by a black *mantili,* clasping their hands in a gesture of woe, female mourners moved slowly toward the deceased. The men folk, soberly dressed in worn but clean jackets, and their faces and hands scrubbed clean, followed.

The mourners crossed themselves and then kissed the small icons on the table. Several kissed my father's face and hands. Others reciting the Lord's prayer, or simply bidding him a fond farewell. Some of the women lingered at Father's side, engaging in what looked like a conversation with the deceased. Although visitors came throughout the day, most came in the evening, after people had returned home from the fields.

Wearing long black robes and a tall rimless black hat, with a large pectoral cross hanging from his neck, Father Manolis came by the house each day. He would bow upon entering. We would respectfully kiss the top of his right hand. He would then attend to Father. While swinging a burning censer over the body three times—symbolizing God the Father, Son, and Holy Ghost—he would intone, "May God forgive the forgiven his sins and accept his soul into heaven for everlasting peace."

The Father prayed. He read from the good book. He made the sign of the cross over and over. One could see his lips moving in silence praying to God on behalf of the deceased. When he finished, he'd bless my mother— and the rest of us, too—with the censer and three fingers of his right hand; again, representing God the Father, Son, and Holy Ghost.

And, we bowed and kissed his right hand, just like we had before. Then he would take his leave. This ritual was repeated day and night over the space of three days. The wake was an intense, painful—and, hopefully, cathartic experience in helping us deal with Father's loss.

Relatives showed up early on the day of the funeral. Soon, more and more people arrived, some waiting outside our front door for the funeral procession to begin. By this time our family's grief was even more palpable. I felt empty, lost and confused. It took all that I could muster just to go through the motions. I felt so ill at ease, so sad.

While the women stood aside, my uncles George, and Strati, and my two brothers, Yianni and Gus serving as the pallbearers, gently lifted the white cloth from under my father's body. They lifted the corpse and lowered it inside a simple pine coffin. They then picked up the coffin, walked outside, and lead the funeral procession of over two hundred mourners to the local church. A long black line filled the main road to church. Church bells tolled as we slowly walked to the cemetery a half mile away. My mother, of course, was sobbing; my sister and maternal aunt held her by each arm as she followed her dead husband. Head cast down, I clutched my sister's hand, bereft. The only sound one heard was that of people crying.

Father Manolis was waiting for us just inside the dark, massive, doorway when we arrived at the church. He bowed briefly and then, swinging the censer to and fro, blessed in turn my father's body and the mourners. The pallbearers walked the coffin inside and carefully placed it on a large white draped table, in front of the altar. Three large white candles in bronze holders, and tied with black cloth ribbons, were placed at the head of the coffin.

I had been in God's house too many times to count, but this time it felt different. I looked around the church walls. The Byzantine icons depicting stern, judgmental images seemed to come vividly to life. God seemed to be staring down at us reprovingly from the vaulted ceiling. The figures in the stained glass looked as if they might speak to me. The smell and smoke of burning incense engulfed the chapel. We were indeed in God's presence! Sunlight filtered now into the cold, gray, smoky space adding a welcome touch of warmth.

With the cantor standing beside him, Father Manolis began service.

"*Kirie Eleison, Kirie Eleison, Kirie Eleison, Doxa se o Theos, Kirie Eleison,*" he chanted, crossing himself.

We stood close to the now open coffin. I found a place between my mother and Gus. We bowed our heads. We held on to one another, trying to hold back tears, albeit unsuccessfully.

I was still in a state of disbelief; just going through the motions. I figured I should stay out of the way, not cry, not draw any attention to myself. Staying out of the way—an admonition I'd heard throughout my life—was my way of being helpful. I actually found it rather advantageous at the moment. It kept me at a safe distance, not needing to engage anyone, or feel the great emotional pain I kept locked inside.

After much burning of incense, crossing ourselves, kissing of icons, pleading with God to forgive Father his sins, we all took turns saying goodbye for the last time. I kissed my father's face and his cold, stiff hands.

"*Yiasou baba. Se agapo.*" Goodbye daddy, I love you.

Although it lasted just an hour, the service seemed to go on forever. I was overcome with grief.

The pallbearers carried the coffin to the cemetery behind the church. The grave had already been dug. At the sight of this deep, dark hole, I could no longer manage my sadness. I broke down and cried. My brother Gus reached for my hand and squeezed it tightly. His eyes met mine, letting me know that he felt the same.

The coffin was lowered into the grave. With trembling hands, we picked up soil and tossed it gently onto the coffin. Then folks started to leave. They hugged my mother, brothers, sister and me, saying "*zoe se sas.*" Mother lingered for awhile. But she gave in to gentle entreaties and was led out of the cemetery. Before leaving altogether, she cried out and muttered something to her dead husband. I looked back one last time, waved wanly, and wiped away my tears with the back of my hand. The grave diggers appeared. They began shoveling dirt onto the coffin.

We made our way back home. Uncle George was supporting my mother, while we walked beside her. Gus continued holding my hand, a gesture for which I was grateful.

Tables had been set in the courtyard to accommodate everyone, including the priest and the cantor. Bread, wine, and a variety of dishes had been placed on the table. A special bread—*prosogio*—was baked for the occasion. Symbolizing the sorrow that attended death, it was made with flour, water and yeast only. *Koliva*—boiled wheat mixed with raisins, pomegranate seeds, powdered sugar and ground sweet croutons—symbolizing the resurrection of the spirit to heaven was also on the table. The *prosogio and koliva* had been blessed earlier by Father Manolis. There was ample wine—my father's wine—for everyone. Before we could eat, the priest stood, and again blessed my father's soul. He went on to bless in turn the meal, our family, our relatives, and everyone who had gathered to mourn Father's passing.

Considering the circumstances, we didn't have much of an appetite. Of course, those not directly affected by father's passing dug in. Some folks exchanged a few words, mainly urging God to forgive the forgiven his sins and accept his soul into heaven.

It was late afternoon when the last of our guests left. Relieved that the ceremony had ended, we were now confronted with the stark reality; Father was gone and he wasn't coming back. His passing would affect our family for years to come.

A Disturbed Family

The alleged suspects were soon picked up by the police and placed under arrest. Included were Kalimanis, the old man, whose age was reported to be one-hundred-two. He suffered from both alcoholism and dementia. He was a small, skinny man with long, wispy white hair and a beard. To me he looked like a ghost, and I was always very frightened of him. I avoided him at any cost. I could never gauge his temperament. He was given to fits of anger, shouting and talking to himself, especially when he was drunk. He would walk the streets barely able to stand. He sometimes used a long, crooked walking stick to stay upright. He would often raise the stick off the ground and point it in all directions, shaking it threateningly at imaginary foes.

His daughter, Panagiota, a stocky woman in her fifties with long, coarse, graying hair was also a sinister force. She was an angry looking woman, who was frequently heard ranting and raving about something or other. She screamed at her family, particularly at her father, and anyone else who crossed her path. She, too, was an alcoholic, and rumor had it that she was "*treli,*" crazy.

She stayed close to home, and didn't mingle with the neighborhood or the community. I often felt more frightened of her than of the old man, for I sensed her deep rage. Thankfully, she didn't venture outside of the house much. Whenever I happened to see her, I made sure to keep my distance.

As for Petros, Panagiota's middle aged husband, he was a total mystery not just to me but to the entire village. Apart from being painfully withdrawn, he appeared not to have either a drinking problem or any noticeable emotional disturbance. He kept mostly to himself, kept his head down, and avoided eye contact. He even appeared to be alienated from his own family. Darkly handsome, he looked more Middle Eastern than European. He seemed to acquiesce to his wife who was obviously the strongest member of the family. I'm not sure where exactly he came from; he had moved to the village when he married "Godzilla."

The couple had two sons who were in their early twenties. Although physically attractive—tall and slim with black hair and eyes—and a gentle, sensitive demeanor, the locals believed that they too were mentally ill. Like their father, they were exceedingly withdrawn. They didn't work, go to school, or have friends; they just stuck around the house.

This very sick, violent family lived in the house behind ours. As far back as I can recall, we were witness to their frequent arguments, physical fights, and drunkenness. We would shut our windows and doors to block the shuddering noise coming from their direction.

Their house was in a state of great disrepair. It had not been painted for years; the old paint flaking off. The wooden fence around the front yard had missing planks and was about to collapse. There was an air of fear and dread about the house, not to mention the family itself. Strangely enough, no one—including my own family—complained about them. No one filed a formal complaint against Panagiota for physically abusing her father; this was something she did at least once a week. Their immediate neighbors, and the town for that matter, simply tolerated them.

When word got out that my father was planning to enlarge our house, the old man, his daughter and her husband threatened him with physical harm. They believed—erroneously—that their view would be obstructed; at least that's the reason they would give.

My father offered to show them the design plans which clearly demonstrated that their view would not be affected. It didn't matter. They continued threatening my father—even threatening to shoot him if he followed through with his plans. As was typical of Father, he secured the necessary building permits and proceeded with the planned construction despite the warnings.

I don't know if my parents ever discussed the threats; I don't know how seriously they took them. Who knows? Perhaps they just dismissed them out of hand as the mad ravings of a group of very deluded people. Sadly, I had also come to understand that it was typical of our family to avoid discussing serious issues. This lack of openness, as it were, prevented serious dialogue of a kind that might have resulted in a solution to the problem our neighbors posed. Moreover, it kept us apart, which increased feelings of worry and anxiety.

By not talking with one another, we lacked the familial support that we so much needed. It seemed to me that my parents believed that if we didn't talk about our problems, they would miraculously vanish. Whenever there was an attempt at family dialogue, my mother would actually say, "Shhh, let's not talk about it." Incredibly, she believed discussion would make problems bigger, less manageable. Thus, her solution to every single problem was to remain silent. If, for example, Gus, wanted to discuss something important, she would literally leave the room. Considering this family dynamic, I don't really believe that my parents ever seriously discussed the threats.

The crew arrived early on the first day of construction. My mother, father, Niko and Effie were there that morning. Gus and I were at school; not sure where Yianni was. According to my mother, the morning began pleasantly enough.

"Kalemera pedia." Good morning men, Mother greeted the crew.

She offered them hot tea, freshly baked bread and cheese. The crew was jovial.

"Ti kanete afentiko?" How are you boss?

Everyone was in a good mood. As the clock ticked on, toward the latter part of the morning, while everyone was busy working, the shutters and window to the neighbor's house facing the work site were surreptitiously opened. Hearing the shutters creak, the workers looked up and saw the old man in the window holding a rifle. Within seconds, before anyone had time to react, the rifle—its barrel now hanging half-way out the window—was fired. Two shots rang out. The first bullet hit my father just to the left of his heart, killing him instantly; the second bullet hit Niko in the left temple, gravely wounding him. Father and son fell to the ground bleeding.

"Katou! Katou! parakalo, katebete katou!"—down, down, please get down, the workers shouted. Everyone dropped to the ground, afraid that they too would be shot. My mother and sister were hysterical. They rushed to my father and brother. Seeing that Niko was still alive, they made sure an ambulance was called. It was too late for Father. He died instantly. Both women knelt over his body, sobbing hysterically. While the workers tried to calm them, gently pulling them away from Father's body, the workers heard the window and shutters above slam shut. The murderers had disappeared into the darkness of their sick, wretched home. Everyone was in shock, they couldn't believe what they had just witnessed.

"Ti egine etho Thee mou?" What happened here, my God?

The crew stated categorically that, although old Kalimanis was holding the rifle, they saw Panagiota standing behind him, where she aimed and pulled the trigger. Murder—virtually unheard of in Greece at that time— had just been committed in this tiny, mountain village of Greece. It shook the community to the core. For months afterward, the village would try to make sense of this horrific event.

Was it just bad luck that we happened to live next door to this violent, disturbed, family? Was it really as simple and meaningless as that? Why couldn't my parents fully appreciate the threat posed by Kalimanis and his family? Why did they ignore the threats?

We knew, of course, that some folks in the village harbored jealousy and anger toward our family; might similar feelings prompted Kalimanis and Panagiota to murder Father? We did, after all, have more land than most in town. And, my parents had the wherewithal to support higher education for their sons. In the end, was it just plain, old jealousy that lead to Father's murder?

Perhaps it had more to do with both Father's insular personality and his politics. Some folks in Skopi despised my father simply because he was a socialist. Might Father's murder have been politically motivated? Perhaps there had been a conspiracy to murder him.

Father was a stubborn man. He lived according to his own unique set of principles, which in his view justified everything. My father lived in a kind of solitary world—one of his own making—and was thus rather naïve about how the real world functioned. He had been warned not to build, but dismissed the warnings. He figured the house was his; he could do whatever he wished with it. It may be that, by isolating himself, Father protected himself from the burdens of life. Perhaps, because he found it too painful to engage fully with others—indeed with life itself—Father chose to withdraw instead. Of course, one can only speculate as to how my father perceived himself vis-a-vis the community. Could this character flaw have somehow contributed to his murder?

Father's laconic personality fostered a tragic family dynamic—that is, if my family not been constitutionally afraid to discuss the threats, they might have been able to see the situation for what it was; then they might have dealt with it wisely, proactively.

In addition to Kalimanis, Panagiota and her husband were also found guilty. Incredibly, each was sent to prison for only two and a half years. Of course, we objected—furiously. This was clearly a premeditated murder! We looked to Uncle George for answers. Unfortunately, he didn't have any; he just told us to accept what we couldn't change. The old man and his daughter were found mentally incompetent; her husband— though not directly involved—was nevertheless found guilty of being an accessory to murder. Testimony at trial revealed that he had been aware of the plan to murder my father; thus he should have reported it to the police. Furthermore, he could have warned the intended victim; he did neither. Considering the short prison terms, they literally got away with murder.

At the end of their term, they returned home, where they continued as before: alcoholism, domestic violence and untreated mental illness. Naturally, it was painful to live next door to a family that had murdered our father. It was more than my mother could bear. Although Uncle George had assumed the titular role of father figure, as a practical matter, all the responsibility of the household fell to my mother. We tried our best to resume the life we knew when Father was alive. We grew closer in spite of the challenges. The pain of our incredible loss forced us to find some solace among ourselves. We found the support that we desperately needed and worked together to maintain some semblance of our previous life.

Separations

Despite our best efforts, our family gradually disintegrated as a result of Father's murder. When his three eldest brothers—now well established in America after leaving Greece some forty-five years earlier—learned of my father's death, they reconnected with us—and the many other relatives—they had left behind.

Worried about their brother Adoni's family back in Skopi, they made every effort to help us. They'd send us non-perishable food, clothing and cash; their generosity helped out enormously. As time went on, however, they began to encourage us to come live in America; they offered to be our sponsors. The idea of starting life anew in America intrigued my mother. She weighed the pros and cons. She talked about it at length with Uncle George, Niko and Effie. She thought long and hard about the prospect of moving to America. She so wanted to put an end to the legacy, as it were, of Father's death and move on with life. But, she found moving on very difficult, when practically every day she'd see the very people who had killed her husband. This factor, I believe, was most significant in her decision to ultimately uproot her family and cross the Atlantic to a new—and very different—life in America. Another reason, equally important, were enhanced educational and economic advantages her children would have living in the United States. She knew that we were no longer interested in working the family's farm; she, herself, did not want this for us. She hoped that America would offer us better opportunities.

After much thought, Mother finally decided that we would emigrate. To be sure, my siblings and I had mixed feelings about our mother's decision. On the one hand, we were excited by the prospect of moving to America, the land of plenty; on the other, we were apprehensive about leaving the only life we knew. We would surely miss our home, our relatives and our friends. In the final analysis, however, we were grateful that we had been offered a chance to escape.

Moving to America presented certain challenges. The most significant being that we would not be allowed to emigrate as a family. We would have to emigrate on an individual basis. Furthermore, eligibility was limited to children orphaned by the events of World War II. Here too, Mother had a life-altering decision to make. The thought that we would not emigrate together was unacceptable to her, as it was for all of us. Would it be worth it? Naturally, we had no way of knowing for sure.

For his part, Niko very much wanted to move to America. He was eighteen after all, almost an adult. He just graduated from high school; he would have left home in any case, so why not to the United States? Mother wanted to support him in this, but the thought of being separated from her first-born son by a distant and unknown country was hard for her to contemplate. In time, however, typical of our mother, always putting her children's best interests ahead of her own, Mother agreed, that the best thing for him was to start his adult life in America.

With tears in her eyes, Mother made the announcement at dinner one evening.

"I know how much you want to go to America, Niko, and you should; it is a wonderful opportunity for you," she said to him. "I hope that in the not too distant future, we will join you there."

She then picked up her fork and, hands trembling, proceeded to eat her dinner. Glancing at one another first—and without uttering a word—we followed suit. My mother's decision to let Niko go would prove to be a watershed moment for our family. Personally, it made me uneasy; I'd bet it had a similar effect on my siblings.

Mother said very little the rest of the evening. In the days that followed, however, she got busy with the job at hand. She made numerous trips to the immigration office in Athens, and filed a voluminous amount of paperwork. Thankfully, Uncle George usually accompanied her and Niko to Athens, to help navigate the enormous and confusing bureaucracy.

"Did you hear, Niko, the widow's son, is leaving for America?"

Word swept the village. Some folks would stop Niko and Mother in the street, seeking confirmation, and wishing them both "*kali texi*" good luck; others would pass them without saying a word even though they most certainly knew.

There was one more thing that we needed to address, and that was our status as so called war orphans. Yes, we had lost our father, but we were not orphans in the strict sense—and certainly not as a result of the great war. Mother worried that this technicality might prevent us from emigrating. Fortunately, an angel in the immigration office in Athens looked kindly upon this middle aged, black clad, seemingly poor woman and advised my mother to list my siblings and me as war orphans. For some time afterward, Mother remembered this kind soul in her prayers at night.

So, the first person to leave for America, of course, was Niko. He was the first to "cut the cord," as it were. He was sponsored by Uncle Bill, who, along with his brother Charlie, lived in San Francisco. Apparently, the brothers had had a falling out, and Bill and Charlie left New York for San Francisco and Tom moved to Detroit. Uncle Bill was well-off, having made a fortune in real estate and the stock market. He was married to German born, controlling Gertrude. They had two adult children, Billy Jr. and Helen. Uncle Charlie married the very attractive Katerina, Kay for short, a Panama-born Greek woman. They had three teenage sons, John, Tom and Tony. Uncle Charlie wasn't as lucky as Uncle Bill in either business or the stock market. He provided well for his family, however, operating a successful neighborhood grocery store. Uncle Tom married the tempestuous Antoinette—also known as Anna—an Italian-born woman from a wealthy family; they had no children. A stationary engineer, Uncle Tom was the only brother who could legitimately claim to be a professional.

Niko left for America on a smoldering hot summer's day in August. It was very hard for Mother to see him go—as it was for all of us. We took comfort, however, in the knowledge that one day we would all be together again. We cried as we bade him farewell; indeed mother wouldn't stop crying for the next several months, she missed her son so. When we tried to comfort her, she would deny that she had been crying.

"I'm all right. No need for you to be concerned. Go now."

If we persisted, she'd raise her arm shooing us away. We felt for our mother, but she obviously didn't want to talk about her pain. If, for our sake only, she tried her best to wear a brave face.

To my brother's credit, he wrote often, which was a great relief for Mother. He had good news to report—he was happy, he liked living in the United States, and enjoyed living with Uncle Bill and his family. Uncle Bill offered him work in his grocery store business. He would eventually become a butcher, a full-fledged career for Niko. He soon began including cash with his letters, sending anywhere between twenty to one hundred dollar bills at a time. It sure looked like Niko's immigration to America was indeed successful. Mother would read his letters over and over and would take pencil to paper and write back immediately. Niko's correspondence was a godsend for Mother; it helped alleviate the pain of his absence.

On his way to San Francisco, Niko stopped in Detroit to meet and visit with Uncle Tom and Aunt Anna. My brother learned that Uncle Tom worked for an automobile manufacturing company named Gemmer. A registered nurse, Aunt Anna worked for Detroit General Hospital. They lived in a beautiful, two story brick house on Detroit's east side. They were in their late fifty's and quite an attractive couple, my brother wrote.

Niko described Uncle Tom as being a tad over six feet tall with broad shoulders and a full crop of wavy, gray hair. He had a handsome square face and the familial hooked nose. An easygoing sort, Uncle Tom still spoke Greek well. He still practiced some of the same customs he had grown up with as a child in Greece. He loved Greek food which he and his wife would frequently prepare, especially roasted leg of lamb and potatoes. He and Aunt Anna would frequent their favorite Greek restaurant—The Greek Taverna—on Monroe Street in Greek town. He had numerous records of traditional Greek songs that he'd often play, singing and humming along.

For Uncle Tom, Niko's visit brought back many fond memories of growing up in Greece. He happily shared those recollections with his wife and nephew. Recalling his friends from childhood, he asked if any of them were still alive. He listened intently as Niko talked about family and about Skopi. My brother became a kind of link, as it were, to a past Uncle Tom had long forgotten.

Almost fifty years ago, around the turn of the century, and during a time of European migration, Uncle Tom, then fifteen, his father and two younger brothers had sailed for America. Uncle Tom's father stayed with his young sons in America for a few years before returning to Greece, where he fathered still more children. Although the old man traveled to America a couple more times to visit his boys, contact eventually stopped—that is, until news of my father's murder made its' way to America.

Aunt Anna stood about five feet four. She was attractive, had a voluptuous figure and porcelain like skin. She typically pulled her fine white hair into a bun. There was a certain aristocratic air about her, Niko wrote. She came from a well to do family. She immigrated to America with her family upon the unexpected death of her very successful businessman father.

According to Niko, their marriage was not exactly a happy one. They came from different cultures, and apparently from a different social class as well, and that seemed to matter to Aunt Anna. She was high-strung, nervous, and unhappy. She was especially unhappy that they had not been able to have children of their own. To help fill the void, they took in foster children over the years and helped raise Aunt Anna's two nephews.

Still desirous of a child despite her age, Aunt Anna became very excited when Niko talked about his family back in Skopi, especially the fact that he had a little sister—*yes, that would be me*—with blond hair and blue eyes. She inquired as to the possibility of sponsoring me; she was eager to start the process of bringing me to America to live with them as soon as possible. Although Niko worried that I was still too young to leave the family, he, nevertheless, conveyed their wishes in one of his letters to Mother. Like all major decisions, Mother gave this much thought, deciding at the end that at age of nine, I was too young to leave home, and that we should wait couple of years—perhaps when I was eleven or twelve years old.

Effie's Wedding

As it was customary in many parts of Greece, especially in small towns in the 1950's, young people were neither permitted to date nor to arrange their marriages. Effie, then in her mid 20's, well within the marriage age, and her intended had known one another all of their lives; they were born and raised in the same village. Unbeknownst to family, they were enamored with one another but they needed to keep their feelings under wrap until the appropriate time.

A marriage proposal was initiated by a—*sibetheros*—a trusted friend of the prospective groom. He would come to the door bearing the customary tray of pastries. If the young woman and her family were receptive, they would send word back with the *sibethero*. A meeting would then be arranged to discuss the serious matter of a dowry. Dowries typically comprised of a mix of cash, real property, furniture, and a variety of linens the young woman had made over the years in anticipation of this very day. By this time, Effie's hope chest overflowed with everything a young married couple would need to start their life together.

"Greetings, Mrs. Siakotos, how are you on this beautiful day?" said Pericles—the *sibetheros*—when Mother answered the door.

"I bring a message from Nick Sideris and family. He would like to ask your daughter's hand in marriage, if that is permissible with you, of course." He looked at my mother with searching eyes.

"Please sit down," said Mother, ushering him inside. "May I bring you something?"

"By chance do you have any wine left from the vintage of the late and forgiven Adonis?"

"I believe we just might."

Pericles sat down at the wooden dining room table and made himself comfortable. He tugged at his worn jacket, and ran a hand over his dusty, black hair. After looking about the room, he folded his hands and waited patiently for Mother's return from the kitchen. A few minutes later Mother entered the room balancing a tray on which she had placed a glass of red wine, a small plate of feta cheese, a small bowl of olives and homemade bread. She placed the tray on the table.

Hesitating for a couple of seconds, he then reached for the wine. Raising his glass, he said, "Here is to our health, and maybe to a future wedding?" again looking at my mother, searching for a clue to what she might be thinking. He took a deep gulp of wine, sighing in delight. Wiping his mouth on his sleeve, he then said, "The late Mr. Adonis, he sure knew how to make wine! May God rest his soul."

Bowing slightly, Mother thanked the *sibethero* for his good wishes. He helped himself to more wine and food. Seeing that her guest was preoccupied with the refreshments on the table, Mother excused herself and went to the kitchen where she found my sister eavesdropping behind the closed living room door.

"You know who is in the living room, don't you?" Effie nodded, trying to control her excitement.

"What shall I tell him?"

"How much do they want?"

"The dowry has not been brought up, but I am sure it will, soon enough."

They looked at one another, their minds already made up

Mother walked back to the living room with a serious look in her eyes.

She was already steeling herself for the dowry negotiations that would soon follow. Our visitor was by now feeling quite relaxed and happy, as he had drunk all the wine and eaten everything on the tray.

"Please tell the Sideris' family that we are honored by your visit, and that we are looking forward to meeting with them—say, tomorrow evening?"

The *sibetheros* quickly stood up, wiping his mouth with the cloth napkin, followed by his shirt sleeve, as a good measure. He assured my mother her message would be delivered promptly.

"*Yiasou, yiasou,*" they bid one another good day. Mother and Effie watched the *sibethero* hurry down the narrow street, humming a wedding tune, before disappearing around the corner.

With a twinkle in their eyes, the two women looked at one another; *so far, so good,* they thought. They knew Nick Sideris was a good catch.

"If only your father and Niko could be here to help us with the dowry negotiations," said Mother wistfully.

"Don't worry, mamma. Uncle George will help us."

Mother would grow sad whenever she thought of her dead husband and her absent oldest son, and for a brief moment she retreated into her own thoughts.

The *sibetheros* was back before nightfall.

"Everything is set, Mrs. Siakotos. The Siderises will be here tomorrow, early evening." Before Mother had a chance to respond, he was gone.

Mother and daughter immediately flew into action. They moved the rag rugs that Mother had stitched together some years earlier to the balcony; they then swept the entire house. They dusted the furniture and washed the windows. They shook the rugs several times, and placed them carefully back on the floor. They straightened the airy, white curtains. Effie took out her best table linen from her hope chest and covered the dining room table. The white table cloth boasted embroidered Greek classic vases at each corner. Effie had used white and blue thread, reflecting the national colors. She looked at it for a moment, admiring her work. I remembered watching my sister a couple years earlier embroidering this very piece. I thought that someday I might embroider a similar table cloth for my own hope chest. As it had never been used before, it was crisp and new and smelled of moth balls. Finally, they placed a vase of flowers on the table.

They set the table. They counted the dining room chairs to be sure there would be enough and arranged them around the table. They settled on the menu: the customary *mezes,* of roasted lamb, a village salad, feta cheese, olives, fresh homemade bread and a carafe of Father's homemade wine.

They watered the sweet basil, oregano, peppermint and marigolds on the terrace. They swept and washed the courtyard. At last, they felt satisfied that the house was ready for this most important event.

Just before the Siderises arrived, they washed their hands and face, and changed into their finest dresses. Finally, having brushed their hair Mother and Effie were ready to receive the *sibetheri,* as they were called.

The sun was beginning to set, casting a golden shadow on the horizon. A light breeze cooled what had been a hot, humid day. Folks were returning home after another hard day in the fields. One could hear the familiar late afternoon soundscape: villagers, children, horses, mules, donkeys, and barking dogs.

Folks lit kerosene lamps, fed their animals, and, exhausted after a long day, disappeared behind their courtyard doors. After a light dinner, they would rest their tired bones and calm their minds before they faced another day tomorrow.

There was a knock at the door. Mother, Effie and Uncle George—who had arrived about a half an hour earlier—stood at attention. Then, Uncle George calmly walked to the door and opened it.

"Good evening. How are you? It is very nice to see you. Please come in."

"Thank you. We are fine. And you, how are you?"

"Wonderful, thank you," the families exchanged greetings.

Seated on the floor by the living room door quietly entertaining myself, I watched as negotiations began. It was rather like watching a sporting event.

After the preliminary pleasantries, wine and food, Mother began by saying, "Effie is a lovely young woman who comes from a good family. She will make a good wife, and God willing, a very good mother. As you know, I am a widow and have four other children to support, including another girl who will need a dowry of her own in the not too distant future." She paused, to let her words sink in before starting again.

"Eighteen *stremata* of land, two-hundred and fifty *drachmas*, and every household item the young couple would need to begin married life together."

She paused again before declaring: "This is my best offer."

Turning their chairs to face one another, the Siderises huddled together to discuss Mother's offer. Deeming the offer insufficient, they counter-offered.

"Twenty-four *stremata,* including the *Pegadi,* and three-hundred *drachmas,* half of which to be in gold coins. The household items you mentioned are, of course, to be included."

"You are asking too much. As I have said, I have other children to consider." I could hear—and presumably so could the *sibetheri*—the annoyance in Mother's voice.

"I appreciate your situation madam," replied Mrs. Sideris. "But you must understand your daughter will not only be marrying the handsome— and much sought after—*levendi,* but will also be marrying into a highly regarded family. Like you, I too am a widow and I must consider what's best for my family."

Negotiations continued into the night. Finally, Uncle George, much to Mother's consternation, proposed that the *Pegadi,* be split in two. "It's a large parcel, and can easily be divided in half; moreover," he continued, "it's one of the best parcels we own. It has a well, and it's close to Tripoli. Its location makes the property quite valuable." Alas, Uncle George wasn't done running his mouth.

"We will give you the three hundred *drachmas* you ask for, but only one quarter will be in gold coins."

I could see how frustrated, how angry Mother was getting. She must have been thinking that her brother-in-law was giving away the store, so to speak, but she really couldn't say anything, but to go along.

Nick, the prospective groom, appeared impatient and seemed ill at ease. He tried to move things along, keeping his eye on the main prize— Effie. After several hours of back and forth, they reached an agreement. Fearing that the other might back out, both parties quickly rose and toasted the betrothed.

"*Na zesoun, na zesoun,* " long lives to the new couple.

The men shook hands, the women hugged and kissed. Pastries were passed around, Turkish coffee drunk. I fell asleep to the joyous ruckus in the living room.

My sister was floating on air when I awoke the next morning. Having shed the black, she was wearing a beautiful, multihued dress for her new status, *engaged to be married.* She sang while looking through her hope chest, admiring the clothes, bedspreads, tablecloths, napkins, blankets, sheets, pillowcases, towels she had weaved, sewn and embroidered over the years. She would soon be using them all in her new home. She wanted to air everything out, eliminate any mustiness. Mother and I helped her remove every item from her hope chest. We hung everything variously on the terrace, fence and courtyard wall.

Passersby would "ooh" and "aah" as they went by.

"Did you embroider this beautiful pillowcase? Did you weave this gorgeous blanket? Did you use a pattern, or was this your own creation? My, my, you must teach me to make this very delicate stitch; you must have used the sewing machine? Long life to you and your intended."

Effie and Mother beamed with pride. It was now permissible to announce the engagement to the public. My sister and her fiancé Nick could now be seen out in public together—along with a chaperone, of course.

The job of chaperone fell on Gus. He didn't mind at all; actually, he enjoyed it. He liked Nick very much and enjoyed the perks that came with being a chaperone. My future brother-in-law also visited my sister at the house. He would take her for walks, and squired her to cafes, festivals and the movies.

Mother and Effie took on a fervent pace in preparation for the wedding. They frequently went to Tripoli to purchase every possible thing she would need for both the wedding and her new home. Pots and pans, plates, bowls, silverware, an armoire, and more.

Upon marriage, Effie would move in with her in-laws. She and Nick would have their own bedroom, and a dressing room, but they would share the common areas. Effie would become part of her husband's family, assuming a variety of responsibilities that included cooking, cleaning, shopping, and attending to the land.

A strong woman with high standards, Mrs. Sideris was well known in Skopi for being a difficult personality, stubborn and demanding. Still, it was expected that Effie would be a respectful and compliant daughter-in-law.

In the meantime, Mother was keeping an eye on the budget. She wanted to give her daughter what she needed to start her new life, and to provide for a nice wedding.

We were all happy for my sister, but already we were beginning to feel the pangs of the impending loss. I had a glimpse of what my sister might be feeling, as well. She would often look at me and, patting me on the head, she'd say, "It is okay, I am not going far. We'll see one another as often as we want."

She must have felt feelings similar to those I was feeling—a kind of nostalgia, for lack of a better term—but she had her future to think about. She was in transition, trying to balance the only life she had ever known and a new life she was about to embark on.

Effie and I weren't all that close. We had different personalities, different temperaments, and she was much older than me. Still, I knew I would miss her very much.

Before we knew it, it was her wedding day! Relatives from as far as Athens and Salonika were invited. Some guests arrived the night before. It was lovely seeing relatives that we had not seen in a long, long time. We had so much to catch up on. It got pretty loud at the house, what with everybody talking at the same time, and laughing loudly. Naturally, Father's death came up in conversation; folks remarked how sad it was that he wasn't here to enjoy his daughter's wedding and to give her away.

"Where is Adonis?" they would ask. "He should be here today!" Making the sign of the cross, they would say, "May he rest in peace."

His passing was still a touchy subject for all of us. One could see it in our eyes, feel it in our presence. Thus, discussion of his death was kept at a minimum. The focus was fixed on the happy event we all had gathered to celebrate.

We were all up before sunrise on the day of the wedding. With such a crowded house, we all took turns using the meager bathroom facilities. We dressed in our finest and prepared to enjoy this wonderful summer day, my sister's wedding day, to the hilt.

Someone turned the phonograph on. Traditional wedding songs

filled the room. A few people started to dance while we waited for the bride to emerge from her bedroom, where my mother, cousins and close friends were helping her with her gown. She finally came out, looking just stunning. She wore a beautiful, floor-length white gown with a sweetheart neckline and long sleeves. She accessorized it with a pearl necklace, tear drop earrings, and white gloves. Red rouge and matching lipstick added color to her already flushed face. She had pinned up her lustrous brown hair. She appeared a little apprehensive; we figured it was just the normal bride's jitters.

"Turn around, and let us see how beautiful you are," we cheered her on.

Turning around, Effie broke out into a broad, beaming smile.

The sound of galloping horses momentarily distracted us from the beautiful bride. The groom, his best man and ushers, had arrived to pick up the hope chest and other wedding gifts. I must say, the handsome riders and adorned horses rivaled the lovely bride. The horses' manes, thoroughly brushed, glistened in the bright sun. Brilliant tassels hung from their bridles, long ribbons from their tails. Beautiful, multi-hued blankets—the bride's blankets—were thrown on their backs. The horses were now standing on their hind legs, neighing and looking quite dramatic. In total control of their charges, the riders throbbed with pride and virility. They looked positively gorgeous in their brand new dark suits, white shirts, and black patent leather shoes. A festive, almost surreal piece of theatre was being played out before my astonished eyes.

I was so excited by this cavalcade of sound and vision that I wanted to get up and dance, but I didn't have the courage. Instead, I clapped and swayed gently to the music. I kept thinking how lucky my sister was and that, when my turn came, I wanted a wedding just like hers. It wouldn't hurt either, I thought, if my groom was as handsome as Nick Sideris.

As the groom could not see the bride until he stood beside her in the chapel, we quickly pushed Effie back into her bedroom, while choice items from her hope chest were handed to the four horsemen still on horseback. Laughter and merriment filled the air. Red wine was passed around. Everybody was having an incredibly good time. A reveler toasted the happy couple:

"What a lucky groom! Look at all the beautiful things lovingly made by your bride. You are marrying a talented, hard-working young woman. May God give you both long, healthy lives, and a house full of children." Everyone laughed.

When the entourage couldn't possibly carry another thing, the riders turned their steeds around and happily galloped away. The women tossed flowers at them as they rode off. The horses were loaded with a variety of colorful gifts, a richness of color creating a brilliant tapestry. The remaining gifts would be retrieved after the newlyweds came back from their honeymoon.

Now that Nick was gone, it was safe for my sister to come out and join us. After a few more adjustments to her gown and veil, she was ready to lead the wedding procession to church. She descended the stairs to the courtyard where she paused and looked around.

"Do I look okay?" she asked timidly.

"You couldn't look more beautiful. Now, go and get married, you lucky girl."

On her right arm was Uncle George who would give the bride away. My mother held onto her left arm. With family, friends and village folk following closely behind, Effie, Mother and Uncle George walked in dignified fashion to church.

The church was decorated with baskets of flowers. Ribbons and bows had been tied to long white standing *lambades,* candles. Father Manolis was dressed in his finest, wearing white and gold long robes embroidered with large crosses. A silver cross hung from his neck. His beard was combed and nicely trimmed. His long black hair was wrapped into a neat bun and pinned to the back of his head.

The ceremony began with the Father blessing the bride and groom. He then blessed the guests. He swung the burning incense censer toward the couple and then toward the guests. Everyone bowed slightly to Father's blessings, and then we crossed ourselves. The priest made the sign of the cross and read a passage from the Bible.

The ritual of the *stefana* or crowns is a significant part of all Greek Orthodox weddings. Consisting of two wreaths made of dried white flowers tied together with a white ribbon, the *stefana*—having been blessed by the priest—are first placed on the groom's head and then on the bride's. The best man then crisscrosses the wreaths three times over the couples' heads, before replacing one wreath on the bride's head and the other on the groom's head. With the priest to their right and the best man to their left—and with the maid of honor carrying the train—bride and groom, balancing the *stefana* with bowed heads, walk around a small ceremonial table. This is repeated three times. This rather complicated ritual is meant to commemorate the first time the wedded couple walk hand in hand as man and wife. Then, after the bride and groom receive holy communion, the hour-long wedding ceremony is brought to a close.

Now gathered in the church courtyard, members of the wedding party partaking of the customary sugar-almonds—the symbol of fertility— hugged and kissed. They wished the newlyweds well, saying, "May you have a long and prosperous life—and many sons!" Nick and Effie were flushed with excitement. *Euxaristo, euxaristo,* they made sure to thank everyone personally for coming. Their faces were literally covered with lipstick traces from all the kisses they received. Laughter echoed throughout the church courtyard. It was a loud and festive event, so much so that someone was heard to remark, "I'm afraid we'll awaken the dead." I could easily imagine that very thing: the graves in the adjacent cemetery would crack open and the skeletons would rise. They would join hands to form a circle and dance in honor of Nick and Effie.

After a while, the newlyweds and their guests walked to the Sideris' home, where the festivities continued late into the night. Instead of going with them, our side of the family returned home to resume our own celebration. As unusual as it sounds, this was in fact accepted practice— it symbolizes the bride leaving her biological family, and joining her husband's family. Without the bride and groom, however, it didn't take long for our party to fizzle out. Folks started to leave after a short while. Those who had come from far away would stay the night.

We had a light meal of leftovers, toasted the newlyweds one last time, and bid one another good night. We fell asleep to the sound of revelry— if not down right debauchery over at the Siderises. I fell asleep next to Mother, a little sad at the loss of my big sister, but exhausted too.

The next morning we were up at the crack of down. After breakfast, we said goodbye to our guests. We cleaned the house and the courtyard and put everything back in place. Our nuclear family had just gotten a little smaller. When once there were seven, there were now only four. That number would soon be whittled down to three. Preparations were being made for my departure to America.

Uncle George

My mother received numerous immigration forms from Uncle Tom and Aunt Anna. In order to acquire my visa so that I might immigrate to America, she needed to submit the completed forms to the immigration office in Athens. As in my brother Niko's case, we figured it would take about a year before I would be ready to leave. I was now almost eleven years old. In order to ward off the sadness and apprehension that came with thinking about my departure, Mother kept reminding herself that moving to America—the proverbial land of milk and honey—was a good opportunity for me.

So, with Uncle George's guidance, and generous expenditure of time, the process of jumping through numerous bureaucratic hoops, so to speak, began. Over the course of a year, we made a number of trips to Athens, an experience that overwhelmed and intimidated me.

First, we had to take a bus from Tripoli to Athens, which was a two and a half-hour ride. The very mountainous terrain of the region, and the narrow roads navigating its surface overlooked cliffs hundreds of feet to the sea below. With few road signs, one had to be a very experienced and careful driver, hardly a representation of a local driver. Most people traveled by bus or taxi, often sharing the cab with others. Very few Greeks drove at that time in any case. Driving was both a luxury and a status symbol for those few who were lucky enough to own a car, or who could afford to rent one. Although nerve-wrecking, most people found traveling to Athens by car a pleasant and entertaining experience. Despite the risk, some crazy drivers would even race on the narrow roads. There had been several fatal accidents on the main road between Athens and the Peloponnesus. It was big news, indeed, when a newlywed couple and the taxi driver ferrying them in his brand new Mercedes, died in a crash on the way to Athens. The cabbie had been hired to take the happy couple to Piraeus, the port of Athens, where they were to board a ship for their honeymoon in the Cyclades Islands in the Aegean. Their families were devastated when they heard what happened. Locals were horrified.

The cabbie, apparently, lost control of his car because, it seemed, he was driving a little too fast around the narrow, sharp curves of the road. The car rolled down the mountainside before exploding. Promising themselves and God they'd drive more carefully, the accident and the deceased were soon forgotten, with little lasting impact on young, inexperienced drivers. Impatient drivers would honk their horns and often passing on the wrong side of the road. They would make remarks impugning one's driving and/ or intelligence.

"Get out of the way *vlaka!* fool. Who taught you how to drive anyway?

Go back to driving school, *malaka*. And get a driver's license, why don't you," they would laugh good naturedly.

They'd be busy lighting a cigarette, or playing with their *komboloi*, worry beads. They would sing along with the music blasting out on their car radios—driving safely became secondary.

Most often, we got around by bus. As I suffered from motion sickness, the journey to and from Athens could be a fairly miserable one for me. Just the thought of the big, smelly bus, let alone actually riding in it— made me queasy. Upon boarding, small paper bags were routinely handed out to passengers. Without exception, I would vomit into mine soon after leaving the bus station in Tripoli. My guts would be at my throat pretty much all the way to Athens. I would fall in and out of sleep, while leaning against my uncle's shoulder. He had made this trip so often that it hardly bothered him.

"It's okay, Toula. Just look out, beyond the front of the bus, far out into the horizon. That ought to help." Unfortunately, by then I would be too sick to even lift my head. He would do his best to comfort me, gently patting me on the head.

I loved my Uncle George. He must have been in his mid-forties at that time. He was rather tall, around six feet, handsome, and had a nice build. He had brown hair and blue eyes. And unlike the rest of us, he had long, slender fingers. He preferred dressing casually. He'd wear a white shirt and beige pants and matching jacket. He would forgo a tie if he could help it.

He had a gentle temperament. His eyes were warm and kind. He spoke with a soft but assertive voice. My uncle looked as though he'd been born, raised and educated in Athens. He was brilliant, and well respected throughout Skopi. The town's lone intellectual, he had served as the mayor as far back as I could remember.

Uncle George had never married. Rumor had it that during the civil war he fell in love with a female comrade. Sadly, he had to end the love affair after several years because his family disapproved.

He would spend most of his time in his small bungalow where he did his mayoral work. Folks would go to him with their problems. They were concerned about an array of issues along the lines of . . .

"Mr. George, my neighbor's goat jumped the small fence I had just put up to protect my property. Now, the fence is on the ground, and my vegetables are gone. You must do something!"

"Mr. Nomothetis is trying to steal my land bit by little bit; the wire fence he built last week is clearly on my property. You must do something!"

"I can't walk across town to visit my grandmother because of the vicious dogs running loose. You must do something!"

Uncle George would patiently listen to each person's concern. He would then, in his usual mild manner, and the ever present smile, make visits to each household in question and have a friendly little discussion. Most often, solution satisfactory to all concerned, would be arrived. For those who, even after a lengthy discussion were still uncooperative, a little out of pocket drachmas would usually do the trick.

Uncle George's bungalow included a kitchen, a bedroom, living room and a den which served as a library and office. A grape arbor hung over the veranda. The place had vegetable and flower gardens. A rooster and some chickens pecked about. Every once in a while he would have a sheep or goat. He loved his little pooch.

Although he tended to his house and garden some, most of the work was done by Stella. Short, stout, smart and sunny—and single—she lived next door to Uncle George with her parents and younger brother. Smitten as she was with my uncle, she would do just about anything for him. She was at my uncle's house a lot, ostensibly working. But, folks were beginning to talk.

"What is she doing there all of the time?" neighbors would gossip. "Why do her parents allow a single young girl alone with a much older bachelor? What is wrong with them? Don't they know any better? She's ruining her reputation. No one would take her for a wife, not now. She better watch it," and on it went.

Uncle George put an end to all the gossip by marrying Stella. Still, most folks believed that he had made an honest woman out of her not because he loved her but because she filled a variety of his needs.

"He needs someone to cook and clean for him—not to mention meeting his physical needs—while he pursues his academic and political interests," some locals would say reprovingly. Uncle George took it all in stride. Aunt Stella, as she became known to us, proved in time to be a good wife and a wonderful aunt. They never had children of their own, so they doted on their many nieces and nephews, even sending a couple to university.

It was well known around town that Uncle George was a socialist. He spoke openly of his support for a socialist government in Greece. He was an idealist who truly cared for people's welfare; he felt socialism best served the needs of the people. He practiced what he preached too. Polite and helpful, he encouraged others to behave similarly.

People in town liked him. They would stop by his house for chats. He would receive them in his den. The room was stacked from floor to ceiling with hundreds of books on every conceivable subject: history, science, medicine, mythology, literature, geography, art. People's questions ranged from theology to medicine and everything in between. His door was always open—to friend and foe alike—no matter the need.

Uncle George served in WWII and been involved—at least rhetorically—in the civil war that erupted in Greece soon thereafter. Intellectually, he was in support of the civil war. Although he never formally joined the communist mountain guerrillas, he was indisputably a sympathizer. The government—and even some village folk—were convinced that Uncle George served as a contact person for the guerrillas, communicating and passing information in code. He always denied this.

Having been "wounded" in WWII, Uncle George was discharged from service on disability. His injury was never substantiated. Uncle George claimed to have a heart condition caused by the war, according to him. The veracity of his claim was challenged by both the government and some of his fellow citizens. They accused him of making the whole thing up because he was lazy and didn't want to work. In the end, however, Uncle George prevailed and was awarded a monthly stipend sufficient to meet his living expenses for the rest of his life.

We looked up to Uncle George for he had taken our family under his wing at a time of great duress. I missed having a father, especially when I heard neighbor kids calling out to theirs: *"Baba! baba!"* daddy, daddy.

It broke my heart to watch as the men readily responded, hugging and kissing their children. So, I went ahead and imagined I had a father just like everyone else. Uncle George, my father's younger brother, became my *baba*.

Whenever we went to the immigration office in Athens, we always stayed with my uncle's maternal aunt, a spinster who had a large house in the heart of the city. The house was large enough that my uncle and I could have separate bedrooms. It even boasted an indoor bathroom with a flushing toilet. I had never seen such a wondrous thing before in my life; it took me awhile in fact to figure out how to use this marvel. The floors, kitchen, terrace, stairs, and courtyard of aunt's house were made of marble, a natural resource in Greece.

Uncle George would take me to the National Garden and Zappeio, a sprawling parkland that included a playground, a small zoo, and free-roaming peacocks. He would take me to the famous Plaka for lunch, where I gazed in wonder at the many tourists scaling the unending stairs, and fun-loving locals. Most memorably, we visited The National Archaeological Museum, and the Acropolis. On these day trips, Uncle George would proudly describe the glorious history of ancient Greece and the four-hundred years of unparalleled achievement in the arts, architecture, medicine, sports, literature, philosophy. He spoke about the birth of democracy in the sixth century before Christ. He said that Aristotle had defined democracy "as the rule of many." A government in which the supreme power is vested in the people and exercised by them, Uncle George explained.

He pointed out The Parthenon, The Erechtheon and The Temple of Nike as we walked the grounds of the Acropolis.

He told me that the ancients, our ancestors, had created mythology to explain the unexplainable. Socrates, he said, had held forth in the The Agora, where he gave his daily discourse to the youth of Athens.

He spoke, too, of the philosophies of Aristotle and Plato. All three philosophers identified the underlying principles—the role of reason, how knowledge is acquired, and what knowledge consists of. They understood philosophy to be the love of wisdom, and hence, the birth of metaphysics, epistemology and ethics. The philosophers' attention was on the role of the human being than on the explanation of the material world. He recited from memory reams of text from the plays of the Greek tragedians: Sophocles, Euripides and Aeschylus—their writings reflecting life's tragedies. He remembered parts of Aristophanes' comedy, a parody of life's humor and irony.

Once he even took me to see a production of Sophocles' "Electra" at the famed outdoor amphitheatre at Epidaurus. He explained the genius of the amphitheatre's acoustics, where a drop of a pin on the stage could be heard throughout the theatre.

Although I could not help but share his pride of country, in the gifts Greece had bestowed on the world, I could not quite grasp the significance of what I saw, for I was far too young to comprehend the beauty, depth and complexity of ancient Greece. I was in awe at the miracle of it all, but more than anything, I valued Uncle George's doting attention on me. For him, it was yet another opportunity to lose himself in the richness of ancient Greece, a country that he so loved. He never tired of talking about classical Hellas. This was his passion, I was sure, besides socialism, that is.

The hurly-burly of Athens, a big, congested city, was as overwhelming as the legend of ancient Greece: buses, trucks, cars, mopeds, and the vast number of people buzzing from place to place. In navy blue uniforms and caps, traffic cops stood at intersections blowing on their whistles and swinging their arms, while trying not to get run over.

Athens was hot, humid and smoggy. The sidewalks—and the streets too—overflowed with people. Sidewalk vendors sold *kouloures*—round white bread with sesame seeds—which I never tired of eating. They also hawked nuts, candy, ice cream, and California oranges. Noting the longing in my eyes, Uncle George bought me whatever I had the courage to ask for. My little heart—not to mention my stomach—for the first time felt truly full.

"This is my little niece," he would say when introducing me. "She will be leaving for America soon." Beautiful, sophisticated Athenian women—wearing makeup and perfume—would pat me on the head and wish me well by saying *kalo taxidi,* a safe trip.

All this attention made me uncomfortable. I looked forward to returning home and falling back into the routine of a much simpler, countrified life.

At home, we didn't talk much about the impact of my leaving for America. We attended to the demands of securing my visa and passport, but we didn't speak openly of my eventual departure. Mother was torn about her decision to let me go; I was so young after all. For me, leaving my family and going to America was just an abstraction; I truly didn't dwell on it. This didn't mean, however, that I was above using my impending departure to my advantage. When, for example, my brothers wouldn't let me play with them or their friends, or when they told me to beat it, I would react by saying, "I am going to America, and you are not, so there." These were only words, of course, to give me some sense of power when my brothers hurt my feelings, and nothing more.

My two best friends, Sophia and Vasio, would occasionally ask me, "Are you really going to America?" I tried to dismiss their questions by saying, "I don't know, maybe."

Growing Up

Sophia lived in a fairly big house with a large backyard just down the hill from us. She lived with her elderly paternal grandmother—who was ill with cancer—her parents, two brothers, and a sister. Sophia was the middle child. Like me, she was small of stature, blond and blue eyed. She was a real live wire, always on the go. We grew up together, walked to and from school each day, and were in the same grade. We were fairly good students, but she was not as serious about her studies as I was.

Sophia tended to dominate our friendship. I did what she told me, most of the time, that is. She and I played a lot together. She would frequently come to my house brimming with ideas of fun things we could do together.

"*Yiasou, Toula, eise etoimi?* are you ready, let's go." Before I had time to think, or look to my mother for permission, she'd urge, "Come on, let's go." She was always in a hurry.

With our houses receding in the background, we would walk into the sprawling fields covered in grass, wild flowers, and fruit trees. Skipping happily along, we would stop to pick flowers, and pluck apples and pears from the trees. We would end up rolling and giggling around in the soft grass, just two little girls having fun.

One day Sophia suggested that we take off our clothes. Before I knew it, she was standing naked as a jaybird in the middle of the field. I hesitated, afraid that someone might see us.

"Come on, Toula," she encouraged me on. "Don't be afraid. There's no one around. I wouldn't tell. Promise."

She pirouetted a couple of times before falling to the ground giggling. She was positively giddy. Here was indisputable proof of what I had always known. Sophia was a lot less inhibited than me.

"Sophia, I'm not sure that this is such a good idea."

"Of course it is. Don't be silly. Now, come on. Take your clothes off," threatening to come and pull them off. Finally, I relented.

"Oh, all right. But, just for a few minutes—and remember—you promised not to tell anyone. My mother would kill me if she found out!"

"Yes, yes. I promise. Now, come on. Take 'em off!"

Against my better judgment, I reached for the hem and pulled the dress over my head, placing it carefully on the soft grass. I kept my underpants on.

"Okay, now, take off your underpants."

"Okay, okay. But, just for a few seconds." By this time, I was shaking with fear.

She took a quick look at my body, her eyes finally resting on my breasts.

"You're bigger than me. I knew it, I knew it," she cried out.

"What are you talking about?"

"Your breasts, your breasts, they are bigger than mine."

I had no idea what she was talking about, as I had never looked at myself in the nude before.

"You mean to tell me that you have never looked at your breasts—not ever?" I shook my head "No."

She started to laugh. "You silly girl, look at them. Look at them now—see—and then look at mine. See how much bigger yours are?

"No I won't. And, you can't make me," I stood firmly.

She looked at me quizzically, like she didn't understand what I was thinking, and finally just dropped the subject altogether.

Thank God, the pressure was off. I felt relieved, and made a mental note that when I got home, and no one was around, I would, in private, take stock of my breasts by myself.

I hoped Sophia was right, and that mine were indeed bigger. At that very moment, I felt better than her, prettier than her, a rare feeling of superiority I wasn't used to.

Sophia was busy checking herself out. She raised her arms and craned her neck to see the few hairs growing under her arms. She then looked down at the few pubic hairs sticking up in the air. Though uncomfortable, I forced myself to glance at my growing body.

"I guess we are growing up," I said.

"Yeah, I guess we are." Sophia nodded in agreement.

I had mixed feelings about this. I was already under enough pressure trying to be a good girl. Growing up, from my point of view, meant even more responsibility. Plus, I was afraid that somehow I would not measure up to my parents and everyone else's expectations of me. And, that worried me.

Another time, on a similar outing, Sophia asked that I lie naked on my back on the ground. Again, with great hesitation, I complied once more. Before I could object, she took her clothes off and climbed on top of me—our genitals touching.

"I feel a tingle down there," she said.

"Yeah, I do too."

We jumped to our feet—a little scared, a little excited—and, after a pregnant pause, started to laugh. We would do this a couple more times before losing interest altogether. Instead, we began talking about something we both found much more interesting—boys. We rated the boys in our class and those in the village on a scale of one to ten, talking at length about those we thought were cute and sexy. Now, this was exactly the kind of talk that would have gotten me into a lot of trouble at home, so we promised to keep our conversation between us.

As much as I liked Sofia, Vasio was truly my best friend. As it happened, our mothers were best of friends too. Vasio was smart and fun, and she had a dry sense of humor. She could also be serious when need be. She had brown hair and brown eyes and was rather plain in appearance; she was a little on the stocky side too. We had a lot in common.

She had lost her father and brother in the civil war that followed WWII. Backed by both the United Kingdom and the United States, government forces battled the communist Democratic Army of Greece for control of the country for three years, from 1946—1949. Her father, Constantine—Kostas for short—was a regional commander of communist forces. He and his men always on foot operated from the surrounding mountains. Her father had convinced Petros, Vasio's brother, a handsome young man in his early twenties, to join him in a mission to overthrow the government and install themselves as leaders. They believed that their form of government would better serve the people of Greece. Maritsa, her mother, was vehemently opposed to her son joining up, but there wasn't much that she could do.

The government was determined to capture Kostas and his band of communist guerrillas. In capturing him, they would undoubtedly capture his troops, as well. Their enemy's whereabouts, however, mystified them.

Kostas had kept in touch with his wife on a fairly regular basis. Besides letting her know that they were safe, he would also ask her to send food, heavy clothing for the winter and ammunition. The government, figuring correctly that Maritsa might know where her husband was hiding, proposed a deal.

"If you'd let us know where they are, we will bring them both home safe."

Maritsa worried terribly, especially about her son, certain that he and her husband would eventually be killed. After agonizing over it for some time, she took a chance and accepted the government's offer, and revealed her husband's whereabouts.

"You are giving me your word, you will bring my son and husband safe home?

Do I have your word?" she implored the authorities.

"Yes, yes. Now tell us where we can find them," answered the captain impatiently.

"You also must not let anyone know that I have disclosed this information to you.

Do I have your word?" she again pleaded.

"Of course, of course. Yes. We understand."

At last she gave them the information they wanted. She crossed herself over and over, and prayed to God that Kostas and Petros would be returned to her unharmed.

"I know where they are! The soon-to-be widow told me, poor fool!" the army captain exclaimed to his troops. He knew they needed to move fast if they were to capture them.

Government forces went directly to the location Maritsa had described. The guerrillas were caught completely unaware. And, of course, instead of bringing them home safe as promised, father and son, along with their comrades in arms were shot and killed on the spot. This all but eliminated communist resistance in the region.

Skopi was horrified by the massacre. When it was leaked that Maritsa had been the one that revealed the rebel's hideout, village folk bitterly denounced her as a criminal. They taunted her with threats of harm, and cursed her to the Almighty God.

"Murderer, murderer," they hissed at her. Some people spat on the ground when they passed her on the street. Others gave her reproving glances, cackling bad omens as they passed her by. "May you burn in hell," they screeched at her.

The widow Maritsa, would live with this nightmare until her dying day. My mother, knowing the pain of tragic loss, befriended Maritsa. In time they became friends. They would go to the cemetery daily to cry at their husband's graves. They went to church together on Sundays. Gradually, their friendship grew stronger. They would have one another over for tea or coffee, or a little wine, cheese and home-made bread. They'd share vegetables and fruit from their gardens and sweets they had baked. They went shopping together in Tripoli. As time went on, they would pass the time sharing stories, indulged in a little gossip, and learned to even laugh again. They found comfort and safety in each other's company.

The cost of the civil war was enormous. As many as one-hundred-fifty-eight thousand Greeks lost their lives and hundreds of thousands lost their homes and all they owned. Greek army losses were at eleven-thousand, while thirty-eight thousand communist guerrillas perished.

Confusion vexed the townspeople as to what to do with the corpses left unburied on the mountains. Some folks in town found the courage to go into the mountains and retrieve the body of a loved one. And, to their relief, gave their loved one a proper burial. Others, however, feared revealing publicly that one of their own had been a communist collaborator. Thus, the bodies of many of Skopi's native sons were left to rot in the mountains. As disturbing as this was, those affected believed that they would be jeopardizing their other children if, by going into the mountains, they acknowledged their fallen son's communist sympathies.

The threat—both from the government which routinely rounded up anyone they considered a threat to their control—and from the communists themselves.

Each family had to make its own decision regarding the issue of the massacre. As in most situations, some were praised, while others were criticized. Indecision, animus and grief pervaded the air.

Typically, the guerrillas would come down from the mountains in the middle of the night and abduct young men—and sometimes even young women—especially those whom they thought sympathetic to their cause. They would then retreat to a mountain redoubt, where they would train—and if necessary—brainwash their captives, thus incorporating them into the rebel army.

Since our fathers were avowed socialists, Vasio's family and mine were harshly criticized by many in town. Whenever challenged, she and I would passionately defend our fathers as men of principle with strong idealistic convictions. Having both suffered the loss of a father, Vasio and I understood how the other felt. We supported and encouraged one another. Our friendship deepened as a result. I grew to love and respect Vasio, and I think she felt the same about me.

We stayed in touch over the years. After graduating from high school, she moved to Germany to enter university. She eventually became a linguist in French, German, Italian and English, and taught at the local university. She also served as an interpreter for the German government. She married a German and had a little boy. Periodically, she would visit her family in Skopi. Her mother, now old and frail, was being cared for by her older sister, who had married a local man and had given birth to four children.

As for Sophia, she and her family immigrated to America, settling in Chicago, where she married and had children of her own.

Leaving Home

I had noticed that Mother was not acting quite herself. She seemed quiet, sad, withdrawn. She had difficulty sleeping through the night, often getting up while it was still dark. She pecked at her food. She looked at the few family photographs we had, and placed a couple in an envelope. She bought a small suitcase and a few items of clothing for me, washed and mended my old clothes. Although I noticed this change in her, I never let it get to me—at least not consciously. I simply noted what was going on, and that was all.

It was June, 1952, and already quite warm. In the summer, my siblings and I sometimes slept in the living room or on the terrace. Our small bedrooms would get too hot and uncomfortable. As I had done so many times before, I brought my bedding into the living room and made myself a comfortable little bed on the floor. As she had done on other occasions, my mother slept with me on this particular night. I loved sleeping with my *manoula*. I would feel like a little girl all over again. She did this infrequently, however, for she strongly believed in self-reliance, and as such felt that sleeping with her children would somehow inhibit their developing independence. She made an exception on this particular night, so I cuddled up close to her, and happily fell asleep in her arms.

I awoke the next morning as the sun's rays shone through the living room window. The room felt cool, as the double doors to the terrace had been left open overnight. I pulled the covers up to my chin to keep warm.

Mother was already up. I looked around and saw that on the terrace my siblings were waking up too. They were yawning, rubbing their eyes, and slowly throwing back their bed covers. The birds outside were already chirping. I could hear the neighbors talking, doors slamming, dogs barking—the neighborhood was coming alive. It felt like the beginning of yet another warm, summer day. I had always loved days like this, especially the early morning hours before it got too hot. I loved too that, for a short time at least, we were all together under one roof. Soon enough everyone would leave the house either to go to work or to school.

Rubbing my eyes, I saw that Mother was methodically placing items of clothing in the newly-purchased suitcase. She was crying. What could be wrong, I wondered. Suddenly, I remembered: this was the day of my departure. The day I would be leaving my family, my home, and my country for America. How could I have forgotten? My breath stopped and my heart dropped to the floor. The day had finally come, and I had to confront the reality which I had tried so hard to avoid. But it was true. I was really leaving.

I did not want to go, but what could I do? Everyone was expecting me to leave. Preparations for my departure had been going on for over a year now. I recalled that others in town, including my brother Niko, had already left for America. I really should be grateful, I thought. None of that mattered, however. All I knew was, I did not want to go. I did not want to leave my family, my friends, my school, my teachers, my dog. I could have gone on and on ticking off reasons not to go. Another voice in my head, however, was doing its best to reason with me. It kept saying, *yes, it is very difficult to leave, but you should feel grateful for this incredible opportunity.* I tried listening, tried focusing on my good fortune. I tried gathering the strength to face the day.

Slowly I got up from my cozy little bed and went to my mother and hugged her. I knew that being away from her would hurt terribly. I'm too young to leave my mother, I thought, the knot in the pit of my stomach tightening. I felt nauseous. Tears began rolling down my cheeks, tears that I could not hold back no matter how hard I tried.

Mother tried talking some sense—into both of us. "This is a wonderful opportunity for you, Toulaki. We both should be happy." But, the look on her face told altogether a different story. Crying, we held on to one another for a few minutes. Still, we continued with our day, compartmentalizing our emotions.

Mother prepared breakfast. She cooked homemade oatmeal, fried potatoes, a tomato and cucumber salad, feta cheese, olives, homemade bread, milk and hot cocoa. She made my favorite breakfast, but, considering the circumstances, I didn't have much of an appetite, and neither did anyone else, for that matter. I took my time taking a bath, brushing my teeth and combing my hair. Then I changed into my new black dress and brand new white sandals. But, I couldn't hold back my grief, my sadness. I sat there sobbing all over my brand new dress.

Effie and my brother-in-law Nick arrived. Mother continued with the packing while my siblings and I tried to make idle conversation. It was difficult, as we were struggling with our feelings. The mood, was somber. Our feelings hung in the air—how very painful it was saying goodbye. But there was no question that my going to America was the right thing to do.

Around noon, my American-born cousin John and his friend Harold, who had been visiting relatives in the village, came to pick me up in their rental car. The plan was to drop off the rental in Tripoli, then hire a cab to take us to the port of Athens at Pireaus, where I would board a ship bound for America, and eleven-day journey.

John, Uncle Charlie's son, was in his mid-twenties, tall and handsome. Harold was about the same age as John, but even taller. They had both just graduated from college and had been traveling in Europe before returning to America and settling into careers. John had a degree in business, and Harold in journalism. Uncle George was with them too, acting as translator.

Soon, others—relatives, friends, neighbors—came to say goodbye. With each farewell, my heart broke into ever smaller pieces. My mother—crying and holding me—told me to be strong, to have courage. John tried to lighten things up by telling jokes in his broken Greek. "You know, Toula America is really beautiful. Uncle Tom and Aunt Anna live in a big, beautiful house, and they are very happy that you'll be living with them." Unfortunately, this did nothing to make me feel better.

Before I knew it, it was time to leave. With a heavy heart, I said goodbye to one and all. I literally had to tear myself away, especially from my mother and Gus. My two best friends, Sophia and Vasio, standing at a distance, suddenly ran toward me crying, hugging and kissing me and telling me to be brave. Mother placed my little suitcase into the trunk of the car. As she hugged and kissed me goodbye, I stumbled into the back seat. John got behind the wheel. The car started down the narrow dirt road towards the main highway. Mother held on to the car as long as she could, and then ran after it as it gradually moved farther and farther away from her. I looked back through the rear window—waving and crying uncontrollably—until the thick dust tossed in the air by the moving car prevented me from seeing anyone clearly. My past was being blotted out before my very eyes. The white cloth handkerchief that my mother had given me was already soaked with my tears. Just like that, I had left my village—and everyone I loved—behind. This was more than I could bear.

John described Detroit to me on the way to Piraeus. He told me all about the automobile industry, in which Uncle Tom worked as an engineer. He also described San Francisco and where it was in relationship to Detroit. He talked about his family and Uncle Bill's too. He said I could visit them in the summer when school was out. He even began teaching me a few handy English phrases like "Hello, How are you?" and "Good morning, I don't speak English, I am hungry." He should have taught me how to say, "I want to go home."

I didn't even bother to repeat the phrases, I was so overcome with grief. My spirit broken, I found myself withdrawing. The taxi driver—a young, sweet, funny guy—tried repeatedly to make me feel better during the long trip to Piraeus. He asked me what kind of music I liked and tried to find my favorite songs on the radio. When I complained of nausea, he pulled over and held me while I threw up on the side of the road. He wouldn't get back into the car till I felt better; we would have to stop again and again. He produced a bottle of ginger ale and a box of saltines, his remedy for motion sickness.

"Sip the ginger ale slowly and eat a few saltines; it'll make you feel better."

"Okay, I'll try," I promised. "Thank you."

It was late afternoon when we finally arrived in Piraeus. The port was chaotic, jammed with people. Suitcases of all sizes, boxes tied with heavy rope, and big, bulging colored bags were stacked in heaps on the pier. The cabbie drove around a few times, weaving between pedestrians, before finding a place to park. He jumped out, took my suitcase out of the trunk and placed it on the ground. He looked at me with his kind eyes, then hugged me and said, "Be strong, little one. Remember, you are a lucky little girl! And don't forget Greece."

Having been paid, the cabbie shook my cousin's hand. Then, before getting back into his cab and driving off, he turned and winked at me. As I watched the cab merge into traffic, I realized that I had not learned his name. I did know, however, that I would not forget him.

We now needed to find our friends: Eleni, her uncle and young cousin were to be my traveling companions to New York. It took a while before I spotted Eleni; her uncle and cousin were standing nearby. She saw me at about the same time. We walked toward one another. Eleni hugged me. Her uncle shook hands with my cousin John, and assured him that they would take good care of me.

John suggested that we eat lunch before boarding, but I wasn't hungry. Even so, he went round to the various vendors and bought a number of items he thought I might like and placed them in a bag. The stash included fruit candies, gum, nuts, and *koulourakia*. He gave me the bag, and I held on to it tightly, like a child would hold on to a favorite toy or a security blanket. He also gave me some drachmas. I told him that I had enough money, as my mother and brothers had given me money before I left. But, he insisted, so I took out my little leather wallet and added his money to theirs.

We waited close to an hour to board. Finally, a voice on the loud speaker asked that we all line up for boarding. We were to board alphabetically, based on our last name. Since my last name was Siakotos, I knew it would be a while.

People formed long, rather crooked lines, and waited. Just as I was about to get on the gangway, John handed me my suitcase. Clutching my passport, I hugged and kissed my cousin and his friend goodbye, thanking them both and walked onto the ship.

Yet, another goodbye. I tried, albeit unsuccessfully, not to cry. John and Harold were staying behind to continue their travels for the remainder of the summer. I kept my tear-filled eyes on my traveling companions, who were just ahead of me. We slowly made our way on deck. I felt numb, empty, and very alone. It all seemed so unreal to me. I couldn't make sense of anything. Everything seemed a blur, including my thoughts and feelings.

I heard Eleni say, "I'm going to the cabin. Want to come with me?" I shook my head no, for I was sure I couldn't walk—or do anything else—for that matter. I just stood there frozen. After a minute or so, Eleni took my suitcase and hurried off to the cabin we would share. I moved toward the deck railing and grabbed it, holding on for sometime. I felt hot tears running down my cheeks. I didn't want people to feel sorry for me, so I quickly rubbed my cheeks dry. I tried to distract myself from the incredible anguish I was feeling by looking at my fellow travelers. I saw people's upraised hands waving goodbye to families, friends and country. Like me, some people were crying; others were laughing as the ship's horn sounded, and we began to move away from the dock. I stood motionless, staring out. Then, I, too, began to wave, to no one in particular; I was just waving for the last time, to everything that I loved. While others began moving about the deck as the ship cut to sea, I stood there until I could no longer see land. Greece disappeared from view. I looked around at the ocean surrounding us, feeling devastated.

Eleni's voice broke through the silence. "There you are," she said, looking a little worried. "Come to the cabin, and I'll help you put away your things."

Taking me by the hand, she led me to our cabin three floors below deck. When she opened the door, I saw that there were two small bunks on either side of the room.

"Which bed would you like?"

"I don't care."

"Why don't you take the one on the left?" She suggested.

I plopped myself on the bunk, looking up at the ceiling. I turned and looked out the porthole. I started to cry again. Eleni took me in her arms and rocked me as a mother would her child. She still smelled fresh even after such a long and trying day. She had on a flower fragrance that smelled of rose water, which I liked very much. I'd like to smell like Eleni when I grow up, I thought.

"I know how you feel, Toula. But have patience. In time, you'll feel so much better, trust me." I wondered whether that would indeed be so.

"Do you want to go back on the deck with me?"

"In a while," I said.

Eleni left me alone with my thoughts. I soon fell asleep.

"Toula, Toula, wake up," she said excitedly. "There will be food and beverages available for purchase in the dining room. Get up and wash your face and we will go together and see what they have."

I resisted going because I still felt extremely sad. And, I didn't have much of an appetite. She urged me to get up anyway. "It'll be good for you to get out of the cabin if for no other reason than to get some fresh air."

I got up, washed my hands, and splashed water on my face. I then followed Eleni into the dining room. There were sandwiches, fruit, ice cream, nuts, candy and sodas for sale.

"So, what would you like?"

"Nothing."

"Oh, come now, Toula. You must have something."

I chose to have a cup of vanilla ice cream sundae. She handed me a small wooden spoon. She bought a sandwich, a soda and a pear. We took our meal out onto the deck, where her uncle and cousin joined us. It was beginning to get dark, so Eleni walked me back to our cabin. I changed into my pajamas and got into bed, and started to cry again.

"*Manoula, manoula,* where are you?" I cried out.

One day passed into the next. I desperately wanted to speak to someone about my sadness, about how I missed my mother and brothers. There seemed to be no one in whom I could confide. I thought about talking to Eleni, but decided against it in the end. So I kept my profound feelings of loss and sadness to myself.

I would get seasick for days at a time. I'd spent those days in bed. While in the cabin, I had become aware of a certain familiar and wonderful aroma. It was the unmistakable aroma of a certain Greek cookie Mother used to make. It was the smell of the homemade *koulourakia* which

Eleni had stashed in her bags. Without asking for permission, I began to dig into her sack of *koulourakia*. The wonderful taste of Eleni's cookies comforted me to no end. I continued helping myself every day, sometimes several times a day. The *koulourakia* became a kind of security blanket, a sedative, if you will. They kept me emotionally alive. At the same time, I felt both embarrassed and guilty that I was stealing Eleni's cookies, but I quickly dismissed those feelings. This is a matter of life and death, I thought, half seriously. I hoped that the cookies would last for the rest of the trip, so I needed to monitor myself and not finish them before the trip was over. I prayed that Eleni would not find out that I had been pilfering her *koulourakia* because if she did, she would take them away and I would be doomed. In the end, my prayers were answered. Thanks to the *koulourakia,* I survived the trip. We floated into the port of Ellis Island in New York Harbor eleven days after leaving Pireaus.

New York

It was early morning, June 10, 1952. Eleni was already dressed and about to leave the cabin.

"Get up Toula, and get ready. Put on your nice dress and come up on deck. I'll see you at the usual spot." Then, she hurried off, closing the cabin door behind her.

I got up, washed my face, changed into a dress that I had worn a few times before, put on my favorite white sandals and left the cabin. I walked up the three flights of stairs and found Eleni leaning against the railing at our now familiar spot on deck. On the last day of our trip, the deck was absolutely packed with people, eager to see the magnificent city looming ahead. Commotion, laughter, and excitement filled the air. I squeezed next to Eleni.

"Land, we have arrived—finally! Look, the Statute of Liberty," people were exclaiming.

Even I had heard of the Statute of Liberty. Rising up on my tip toes and craning my neck, I saw the beautiful lady with my own eyes. Holding the torch of freedom, she seemed to welcome our ship to her shores. If I had been asked at that time, I would have said that America was a woman—a mother, really—her upraised hand beckoning her children home. I associated the Statute of Liberty with Demetra—which happened to be my given name. In Greek mythology, Demetra is the goddess of agriculture and fertility—the benevolent Mother.

Despite still feeling sad, still feeling displaced, I now also felt some measure of relief, that we would finally be disembarking after a very long and arduous trip. At the same time, however, I was apprehensive. I knew that my journey wasn't to end in New York but would continue to Detroit, Michigan. Although I didn't know for sure, I sensed that my traveling companions and I would part after going through customs, and this worried me a great deal. I had no idea, of course, where Chicago was in relationship to Detroit—was it a hundred miles, a thousand miles away? What would actually happen once we reached New York City? I was given no information. My mind spun at the thought of yet another ordeal I'd soon have to face. So, I tried not to think about it. I remained in survival mode, just a lost little girl, putting one foot in front of the other, sticking close to my traveling companions.

We stayed on deck, watching the great city loom larger and larger in front of us. I was captivated by the sheer size of the city; it stretched as far and wide as the eye could see. I had never seen so many tall buildings! I looked at the scudding white clouds interspersed with dark vapors discharged by smoke stacks. Lowering my gaze, the city was now so close it seemed I could reach out and touch it. I felt completely overwhelmed, a tiny speck in the middle of an immense world. I looked up at the sky and silently prayed to God to please send a guardian angel to watch over me.

Eleni, on the other hand, was taking it all in stride, seemingly thrilled that our long journey was coming to the end. She tried to evoke that same enthusiasm in me.

"Aren't you happy, Toula, that in just a short while we'll walk off this ship, and step onto wonderful American soil?"

Before I had time to respond to her question, Eleni hurried off back to the cabin to check on our belongings. Like a little dog might follow her master, I was right behind her. We checked our cabin and made sure we were not forgetting anything.

We placed our large suitcases and trunks next to the cabin door, and then rushed up to the third deck again.

The ship had now entered New York Harbor.

On board, the decks were emptying out. A crush of people gathered on the ground level, waiting to disembark. We picked up our bags and joined the others in line. I stuck close to Eleni, Uncle Panagotis and Andreas while holding onto my little suitcase with one hand and to my passport with the other. As the line inched forward, I looked out and saw large crowds waiting to greet families and friends. Again, I felt pangs of longing for my family, but, at least for the time being, I was done crying. It took close to an hour, but, finally, after our passports had been checked, we stepped on dry land. It felt good to be on solid ground again as I had enough of the rolling ocean and the stomach upset it caused me.

Eleni and Panagiotis found their suitcases along with hundreds of others piled on the ground. We said goodbye to a few of our fellow passengers, and then piled into a cab to our next destination—New York's Grand Central Station. While sitting in the back seat with Eleni and Andreas, I listened as Panagiotis spoke English with the cab driver. I wondered what they were talking about, a question I would often hold in mind. I stared out the window at the monumental rise of the city. I had never seen before so many people, so many cars and buildings. The noise was deafening. Like Athens, New York was hot and humid.

As she had been to New York before, Eleni tried giving me a little history lesson, mentioning The Statue of Liberty and The Empire State Building, but, as before, the information was completely lost on me; I just could not process any more information.

After about forty-five minutes of navigating among cars, trucks and busses, drivers frequently honking their horns—and buildings flashing by—we arrived safely at Grand Central. Having retrieved our bags from the trunk, we walked several yards to a non-descript place close to the train

NEW YORK   111

station. Holding my hands and looking straight into my eyes, Eleni and
Uncle Panagiotis gently explained that we would be parting ways here,
that they would be taking the train from here to Chicago, where they
lived. I was to wait for the social worker from the International Institute,
who would put me on the train to Detroit. This news, of course, was
disturbing and I protested. With my eyes welling and my voice breaking,
I tried very hard not to cry.

"It'll all work out fine, Toula. Please wait here at the train station for
the social worker. We wish we could wait here with you, but we cannot
miss our train to Chicago. You understand."

Then, they picked up their suitcases and disappeared into the crowd.

I stood there frozen, my little suitcase, the one constant since I left
Greece, next to me. I didn't know what else to do but wait for the social
worker to come and help me reach my final destination—Uncle Tom and
Aunt Anna.

Frankly, I'm not sure how I felt. I suspect, at some level, I made sure
not to feel anything, for fear that I would surely have fallen apart. Instead,
I got caught up in the incredible whir of activity transpiring in front of
me. Crowds of people were rushing by. I saw people riding up and down
moving steps, and getting in and out small spaces by electronically operated
doors. I saw people going in and coming out multi-level department
stores, holding large, overflowing, bags. I wanted to go into those stores
to buy something to eat, maybe to look at pretty dresses. There might be
toys inside, maybe even a little doll like I always wanted, but never had.
But, I needed to wait for the social worker.

For the first time in my life I saw people whose skin color was different
than my own. I took particular notice of a black man standing alone not
too far from me. He was tall and had on a pinstriped black suit. His black
shoes were really shiny. His close cropped hair was black and very curly.
I thought he looked quite handsome. He was looking straight ahead;

I sensed, that like me, he was waiting for someone. Still, in all, I wondered if I should be afraid of him. But, as he never looked my way, I decided there was nothing to fear. I continued being distracted by what was going on in front of me. It felt like I was at a circus in a make believe city. I honestly couldn't believe that what I was seeing was real. In spite of myself, I found it quite entertaining. At the same time, however, I felt as if I was in my own little bubble, separate from the people around me.

I began to feel hungry and craved one of Eleni's *koulouraki*. Then, I remembered the long forgotten bag of goodies that my cousin John had given me in Piraeus. Searching my suitcase, I soon found the bag. I reached in for a small bag of pistachios; this was followed by a stale, doughnut-shaped bread and a piece of gum.

I don't know how long I'd been waiting when suddenly a smiling, attractive, brunette with kind eyes knelt beside me.

"*Kalosoresate,*" welcome, she greeted me in Greek. "I am very sorry for being late; I got caught in traffic."

Caught in traffic? I had no idea what she meant. She went on to explain that she was from the International Institute and that she was going to help me get on the train to Detroit. Looking around, she saw my suitcase. She picked it up, and took me by the hand. We walked to the waiting train.

She helped me find my seat and stored my suitcase in the compartment above. I held onto my bag of stale goodies, my passport and now my train ticket, which the kind lady had just handed me. She stayed with me for a few minutes and explained that my uncle and aunt would be waiting for me at the *other end*. She then briefly spoke with the conductor and handed him an envelope.

"*Yiasou, k' kalo taxidi.*" She wished me a safe trip, and left.

I liked her, and wished she could have stayed with me a little longer. She was kind and helpful, but I must admit, her Greek was a little unusual.

I had no idea how long it took to reach Detroit; I knew that it was at least an over night ride. Frankly, I hardly remember the trip; I must have slept through most of it. I didn't seem to remember basic things. *What did I eat? How did I get to the bathroom? Did anyone watch over me?* I have no clue whatsoever. Perhaps, God answered my prayers, and had sent a guardian angel to watch over me; it's anyone's guess, really.

Toward the end of what had been truly a surreal experience, the conductor's loud voice woke me with the announcement that we would soon be arriving at Detroit's Central Station. I looked around and saw that I was not alone. A thin woman in her thirties with short, wavy black hair, and a little girl who looked to be around six or seven were sitting across from me. I figured they were mother and daughter. How I wished that my own mother had been sitting there with me! The little girl had a very pretty red gingham dress on. She wore shiny black shoes with a small strap, and white socks that had been folded over, revealing an embroidered rosebud. She was holding a beautiful doll dressed in a crisp white dress. I looked at the white sandals I had worn for the past eleven or so days; they still looked pretty new, I thought. But, I felt uncomfortable in my black dress, which by now needed a good washing.

They were looking at me. The mother, a slight smile playing across her face, seemed friendly enough. The little girl nuzzled close to her mother, clutching the doll tightly to her chest. I never had a doll, I thought. My entire collection of toys consisted of seven marbles. We would throw one marble at a time in the air, catching it in midair while holding the other six in our clenched fist. The winner was the player who caught all the marbles before they touched the ground. I'd played this game with my brothers and friends, and I'd even win occasionally. We also played tick-tack-tow using thin sticks. We did have a deck of playing cards, however, which we played *kolitsina,* a game similar to gin rummy.

I must have drooled at the sight of the doll for soon the little girl handed it to me. I hesitated at first, but then took it. I first held the doll like a mother would a baby and rocked it a little. Placing it on my lap, I began investigating how the doll was put together. I looked at the pretty dress, and under the dress at the doll's underpants, and then under the underpants. I looked at the doll's face, raising its eyelids up and down and running a finger across the thick eyelashes. I patted the doll's wavy blond hair and checked to see how it attached to the scalp. I took the doll's little shoes off and, after checking its feet, put the shoes back on.

I held the doll like a baby again, rocking it once more. I wanted to kiss the doll, but, afraid the little girl might object, I refrained. Soon, she reached out for her doll, and I handed it back to her. I was grateful that she let me play with her beautiful doll. I said *euxaristo*—thank you—hoping that she understood.

The train slowed considerably as we neared the station. The conductor came by to collect my ticket and then withdrew my suitcase from the overhead. Mother and daughter got up from their seats, and I followed suit. We walked down the corridor toward the closest door. As the train came to a complete stop, the door opened. Two hands reached out to me as I got off the train, one taking my suitcase, and the other my hand.

Uncle Tom and Aunt Anna

L ooking up, I saw a middle aged couple. I recognized Uncle Tom from family photographs.

"Hello, welcome" said Aunt Anna, wrapping me in her arms and kissing me on the cheek. She took my hand and held it for a while.

Uncle Tom kissed me too. And as he hugged me, he lifted me slightly off the ground. "How was your trip?" Uncle Tom asked in Greek. I could have explained how long and difficult the whole thing had been, but I just nodded my head, implying that it was okay. He didn't pressure me to elaborate. He just smiled at me sweetly, signaling that he understood, that he felt for me.

I tried resisting a recurring thought: what were my family in Greece and my new guardians here in America thinking in allowing an eleven year old girl to make such a long trip by herself, across the Atlantic Ocean, without knowing a word of English and no preparation whatsoever. For the time being, I suppressed those feelings.

Overjoyed at my arrival, Aunt Anna spoke to me in English as though I could understand her. It made me uncomfortable not being able to converse with my aunt, and wished that she would stop talking to me. No doubt noticing my distress, Uncle Tom interrupted now and again to translate. He then picked up my by-now battered suitcase, and the three of us, a newly-minted family, walked to where the car was parked.

Uncle Tom looked to be in his early sixties. A big man, tall and handsome, he had a full crop of wavy, gray hair and the familial hooked nose. His twinkling brown eyes and broad smile expressed a gentle demeanor. He resembled many of my relatives in Greece; I instantly felt close to him.

Aunt Anna also looked to be in her early sixties. She must have been around five feet, four. She had a voluptuous figure, and beautiful, porcelain, wrinkle-free face. Her white, fine, straight hair was pulled back into a bun. Even though she was smiling, I detected in her affect a stern nervousness. She wore a mauve knit dress, and had a matching bag. I later learned that she had knitted the dress and bag herself, one of her many talents. She had on beautiful diamond rings and a lovely necklace that glittered in the sun. I thought she was very stylish. I liked that about her.

Uncle Tom drove a black Buick sedan. Sitting in the back seat, I watched him turn the ignition on and started down the road. I slid from one side to the other in the tan leather seat. I watched the couple in the front seat chat a bit—that is, before Aunt Anna lit a cigarette and Uncle Tom started puffing on his pipe. I was a little shocked to see Aunt Anna smoking. I thought—wow, she'd be judged harshly in Skopi for smoking. But, I liked what I took to be signs of independence and modernity in my aunt. Uncle Tom started singing in Greek, looking back periodically to see my reaction. Aunt Anna looked back at me often as well, smiling and asking me questions. I smiled back. I loved Uncle Tom's so called singing as it took me back to my village for a brief moment.

My mind was buzzing with a million thoughts and questions, while fear and apprehension—feelings that had never completely left me since I left my home—hovered just under the surface. I wasn't all that sure what exactly I was fearful and apprehensive about—apart from the unknown, that is. Given my present mind-set, I'd assume the worse. The only thing I really knew was that I missed home, but I tried hard not to dwell on those feelings.

While looking out the window at the motor city—at the smoke stacks, at traffic, at the high rises—I wondered what my new home was like. Would it be at all similar to my home in Skopi? Would I like it? Would I have my own room? How am I ever going to manage? I felt myself diminish into a helpless little girl, but I didn't stay there for very long. I had—by now realized—that being strong made me feel more in control. Strength became my coping tool.

My thoughts were interrupted by the growling of my stomach. I honestly couldn't remember the last time I had eaten. I hoped that there would be food ready when we reached the house. With any luck, my favorite dish of roast lamb and potatoes with lots of feta cheese and olives, would be waiting for me.

After what seemed like a long drive, when in fact it was only about a half hour from the train station, Uncle Tom turned down a residential street with mostly large, two story, A-frame, brick homes. Each home had a manicured front yard which included a large pine tree.

Halfway up the block Uncle Tom turned into the driveway of their home. He drove to the back of the house into the garage and turned the engine off. While holding the car door open with one hand, he helped me out with the other. The first thing I noticed was the beautiful backyard, a lush green lawn surrounded by flowers and rosebushes. I sniffed the roses' delicious fragrance. A wire fence covered in sprawling grapevines from which large clusters of dark red grapes hung, separated their home from the house next door.

There was a vegetable garden too. Sunflowers and marigolds surrounded patches of lettuce, cucumbers, tomatoes and zucchini. String bean plants were tied to wooden poles. There were about a dozen corn stalks, two or three corn on each stalk There was an apple tree just behind the vegetable garden, its branches holding what looked like hundreds of green apples.

Wooden posts supported the fruit laden branches.

Looking beyond the limits of my aunt and uncle's house, I noticed other houses on both sides of their home. They were older homes with mature vegetation which lent them an air of stability and history. A few of the neighbors were out in their gardens enjoying the day. They looked like my aunt and uncle, that is, in terms of age and stage in life. Their productive years now behind them. My aunt hustled me over to be introduced.

"This is our niece Toula. She just arrived from Greece."

I detected a slight pride in my aunt's eyes and voice. I was not sure what the neighbors said exactly, but I felt their warm welcome. Uncle Tom reached up and plucked an apple from the tree and handed it to me. I bit into it. It was perfect, juicy and tart.

While we could have entered the house via a small porch in the back, Uncle Tom and Aunt Anna opened the side door next to the driveway instead and ushered me inside. There were stairs to the basement and stairs leading upstairs to the kitchen. Aunt Anna led the way to an intimate, light and airy room.

The square sized room was of medium size. There was a round metal table with yellow trim and four matching chairs in the middle of the room. The tile floor had a checkerboard pattern. A large, gas stove stood on one side of the room, while the other wall accommodated a yellow refrigerator. There were white cupboards, a large white sink, and a countertop made of the same white and black tile on the floor. African violets in bloom were on the windowsills. A wood framed door with glass panes opened onto the backyard. I immediately fell in love with the kitchen.

There was a large baking pan covered in aluminum foil on the stove. I wondered what was underneath. Reading my mind, my uncle asked if I was hungry. He pulled off the aluminum foil. And there it was, a roasted leg of lamb and potatoes! Aunt Anna then took the lid off the aluminum pot on the back burner, and I moved closer to see what was inside.

"It's string beans and tomatoes from the garden," Uncle Tom explained in Greek. My favorite food! How did they know? Who cares—when do we eat?!

While Aunt Anna set the table for dinner, Uncle Tom took me upstairs to show me my very own bedroom. On the way upstairs we walked through the living room, which was furnished with plush carpet, sectional beige couches, and a red leather lounge chair—Uncle Tom's favorite. Then we walked through the dining room which doubled as a family room. It was furnished with beautifully upholstered overstuffed chairs, a love seat, and a rocking chair, its seat and back covered with red, ribbed fabric. This was my aunt's special chair. There was a cabinet housing a small black and white television-set and a stereo system. Leaded glass windows and a heavy leaded glass front door was framed in dark wood. Family photos sat on an elegant wooden mantle above the fireplace.

Uncle Tom led me up an ornate spiral staircase, sliding his large hand along the wrought iron banister. Aunt Anna had placed one of her exquisite porcelain dolls on each step. They were all dressed in beautiful, white dresses and shiny white shoes. Some were standing while others had been placed in seated positions. There were about a dozen. A few had long black hair, rosy cheeks and red lips, while others had short, blond hair. I was surprised—and pleased—to see such a marvelous sight. I pretended that they were all mine, and that I could play with them as long and as often as I wanted. A dream come true. But, I reminded myself that they belonged to my aunt. I hoped that she would let me play with her beautiful dolls.

Upstairs were three bedrooms and a full size bathroom. The first bedroom on the right was my uncle's. It had a large bed, a dresser and a door leading outside to a small balcony. Aunt Anna slept in a separate bedroom across the hall from Uncle Tom's. It was a much larger room with a walk-in closet; it was beautifully furnished. It had a dressing table with a large, oval, leaded-glass mirror where she kept her various powders, lipsticks, a hand mirror, and a beautiful silver hairbrush and comb. On top of the dresser, were an array of perfumes, a package of cigarettes, an ashtray, and a silver cigarette lighter. On each side of her large, high bed, were nightstands on which sat small, crystal beaded lamps. The spacious walk-in closet was filled with dresses, suits, skirts, blouses and too many shoes to count. The picture window was adorned with ruffled, floor length white curtains, crisscrossed and tied back. Venetian blinds provided privacy. Persian carpets covered the beautiful hardwood. It was a magical room to be sure, but why, I wondered, didn't my aunt and uncle share the same bedroom?

The large bathroom at the end of the hall had a standing washbasin, a large bathtub and, as in the kitchen, a black and white tile floor. A light breeze wafted through the small open window.

My bedroom needed some work. It was spacious, but sparsely furnished. There were two windows, one of which faced, pleasingly, the backyard. There was a single bed with a simple wooden headboard, a nightstand with a lamp, and a dresser.

"This was John's bedroom, your aunt's nephew," Uncle Tom explained. "He just got married. Your aunt hasn't redecorated it yet only because she wanted to wait for you."

After storing my suitcase inside the bedroom closet, I washed my face and hands and rushed down to eat. The table was filled with serving bowls and plates of food. Aunt Anna had made a Greek salad of tomatoes and cucumbers with fresh oregano, sweet basil and a pinch of mint. She had also placed on the table a plate of feta cheese, a bowl of olives and a basket of bread. There was water, milk and ginger ale for me, a bottle of Miller beer for Uncle Tom and a glass of red wine for Aunt Anna.

I was seated across from Uncle Tom, facing the door to the backyard.

This would be my seat for the next seven years, the amount of time that I'd spend in my new home. The food was delicious. I ate so much, that my stomach ached. I don't believe I had ever eaten so much before in my life.

It was now quite dark, and I felt very tired; it had been a long day. I wanted to go upstairs to bed. But, Uncle Tom opened the door of the cabinet housing the television and stereo and turned the television on. I was startled by the flickering images on the screen. It reminded me of the few times I had gone to the movies in Tripoli with my brother Gus. Watching the television in my uncle's house felt like being in a little movie theatre. I was very excited and wanted to watch the program on TV longer, but Uncle Tom turned it off and then turned the stereo on. Suddenly, the house was filled with Greek music. He tried to sing along, but only briefly, because he didn't know all of the lyrics.

Finally, it was time for bed. Aunt Anna took me upstairs and showed me how to use the shower and tub. She opened the medicine cabinet and pointed out a few items she thought I might want to use. All I really wanted now was to be left alone and to sleep, for I was exhausted. My aunt pulled a long, sleeveless white nightgown out of the dresser drawer, drew down my bedding, and started to help me get undressed. I wanted to undress myself, but she wanted to help me. I sensed a little tension between us.

Life in America

I resisted getting up. I was too tired from the long and arduous trip. I felt befuddled and melancholy. I missed my family so. I wished I were back home with them. I did not want to begin life anew in the United States. Everything was totally foreign to me. I felt alone and completely out of place. That familiar knot in my stomach, a pattern now, told me that things were not well. I tried to minimize its nauseating effect by not paying attention to it. But hard as I tried, there was no denying the generalized fear I felt.

I tried ignoring my anxiety by listening to the voices coming from the kitchen below. My aunt and uncle, of course, were conversing in English. The beginning of another frustrating day, I thought. I heard my aunt coming up the stairs, and before I knew it, she was in my room, talking away. It didn't seem to matter that I didn't understand a word she was saying. She was in her own little world, oblivious to my feelings. How am I going to survive here, I asked myself.

Aunt Anna, her older brother, Joe and younger sister, Fannie were all born in Italy. They spent their adolescence in Sao Paulo, Brazil. Her father was a successful textile merchant with stores and homes in both Italy and Brazil. Auntie grew up in a world of privilege. Unfortunately, her father died from a massive heart attack when Auntie was barely twenty. This tragic event had a devastating emotional and economic effect on the family; they were completely unprepared to survive on their own. The family fortune was lost. I don't believe my aunt ever found out exactly what happened to it. Suffice to say, her father had been in complete charge; they were irrevocably lost once he was gone.

Like many other families enduring financial hardship in the old world, Aunt Anna's family immigrated to America not long after her father's untimely death. They settled in New York City, where they had relatives. They soon established a successful florist shop. I got the impression that Aunt Anna felt it beneath her and her family to work for a living. On the other hand, however, I could see how proud she felt that they had made a success of the enterprise. How they came to open a florist shop, I couldn't say; I would guess that Auntie's innate creativity might have something to do with it.

I also learned from my aunt that there was a lot of friction within the family, particularly between her and her brother Joe. From the way she described their relationship, and from my observations when Joe would visit, both seemed to be rather stubborn and controlling. The relationship was strained, to say the least, but they managed to maintain obligatory infrequent contact. Joe had remained a bachelor his entire life.

Her sister Fannie had married and had two sons. Auntie described her as emotionally fragile. She suffered frequent bouts of depression. She divorced her husband in time. Auntie helped raise Fannie's two sons, Harold and John. She opened her home to them during the summer months, thus relieving Fannie of their care. Auntie and her siblings would take turns caring for their mother Felomina, an apparently beautiful, retiring and entitled woman. She died of natural causes when she was well into her eighties.

Auntie spoke Italian, Portuguese, and English, but surprisingly, she didn't speak Greek. Auntie met my uncle in New York City. After dating for about a year, they married, and soon moved to Detroit, where Uncle got a job at Gemmer, an auto manufacturing company. He was responsible for the company's heating system. He liked that it wasn't a terribly demanding job. It paid well, and provided excellent benefits. They tried for years to have a family, but sadly, it wasn't meant to be. Eventually, Auntie went to college and studied nursing. She worked as a registered nurse at Detroit General Hospital for many years. Their combined income, substantial for the time, allowed them not only to have a beautiful home, but to maintain a summer house in Port Huron, to own two cars, and to take yearly vacations. Despite material wealth, theirs was not a happy marriage.

Auntie drew down the bedding and helped me out of bed. I wasn't ready to get up, but it seemed she knew better. I went to the bathroom and closed the door behind me. I brushed my teeth, and washed my face. Trying to keep some distance from my aunt, I quickly walked downstairs and looked for my uncle. I found him working in the back yard.

"*Kalemera*,"

"*Kalemera*," we exchanged good morning greetings.

"Did you sleep okay?" he asked.

"Yes, I did."

He continued puttering in the garden. I sat on the back steps, looking out at the thick, newly cut green grass, the vivid dahlias and snapdragons, and the deep red grapes dangling from the fence. Looking beyond the fence, I gazed at the neighbor's equally beautiful gardens. I relaxed in the warmth of the sun, forgetting for a moment my circumstances.

Putting down his pruning shears, Uncle Tom came and sat beside me. "What's the matter, Toulaki?" he asked.

The love and concern I felt brought tears to my eyes, but I held them back for fear that, if I started crying, I would not stop for a long time. I just did not want to feel that vulnerable anymore. I had decided that maintaining a stiff upper lip was the best course of action under the circumstances. I kept the terrible pain of separation to myself.

"I'm okay Uncle Tom."

He looked at me searchingly for a few moments, then, trying to reassure me, wrapped an arm around my shoulders and squeezed me tight.

"After you have your breakfast, Auntie will take you shopping. She'll buy whatever you need."

He picked up his shears and continued with his gardening. Oh, great, I thought sarcastically, yet another encounter with this strange place called America.

I stayed where I was for a while, soaking in the sun.

"Tom, Tom," Auntie called out. "Ask Toula what she wants to eat for breakfast."

"I'm not hungry."

Auntie insisted I eat.

"Whatever is available," I said, getting up from the warm wooden step. I slowly opened the back door and walked into the kitchen. I set in the same chair as the night before.

Opening the refrigerator door, Auntie asked me to pick out what I wanted to eat. I reached for a bottle of ginger ale and placed it on the table. I took out feta cheese, olives, and some watermelon. Aunt Anna must have thought I should also drink milk; she took a bottle out and poured some into a glass. Even though I wasn't hungry, I made myself eat. She sat with me at the table and had a cup of coffee and a cigarette. She and Uncle Tom had had their breakfast earlier.

Feeling listless, I sat a while longer at the table after I had finished eating. A new life, in a strange land so far from home, was just too much for me to bear. I decided right then and there that this whole thing, this entire misadventure, had been a terrible mistake. I will not stay here, I thought to myself, I'm going home. I want my family, I cried inside.

Auntie—unaware to how I was feeling—motioned that we go upstairs. She obviously had a schedule. We walked into the bathroom, where she drew me a bath. I wanted her to leave so that I could get undressed in

private. Luckily, she did. I took my nightgown off, and stepped into the
tub with my underpants still on. How wonderful it felt! I had to admit
that this was so much better, so much more comfortable than the outdoor
metal tub back home in Skopi. I drifted off to sleep.

I'm not sure how long I had been asleep in the tub when I was
awakened by Auntie's hearty laughter. She had come into the bathroom to
check on me and saw that I had gotten into the bath with my underpants
on. She thought that was pretty hilarious. I, on the other hand, thought
I was being modest. Based by her reaction—which, incidentally, didn't
offend me in the least—I figured it was okay both to be in the nude and
to look at myself in the nude. But, I was sure my mother would not have
approved.

Having finished bathing, I stepped out of the tub and into a terry
cloth robe Auntie held open for me. In the bedroom she handed me my
old black dress, which she had washed and ironed the night before. I put
on my white sandals. We were now ready to go shopping.

The light brown, two-door 1952 Ford parked out front belonged to
Auntie. Uncle Tom had just mowed the front lawn, trimming the edges
neatly. Every house had an almost identical front yard. Three tall pine
trees in front of our house provided shade and privacy. At one end of the
broad front porch hung a swing with orange cushions. There were two
metal chairs and a small table on which Uncle Tom's pipe and ashtray sat.
Uncle Tom and Auntie spent many a summer's eve in this idyllic spot,
enjoying the cool breeze and chatting with their neighbors.

To the right of the front door had been hammered on a rock the
number 1929. I now lived at 1929 Sanford Avenue in a middle class
neighborhood on the east side of Detroit. "By the old city airport," Auntie
taught me to say just in case I got lost. "Gratiot, the main street, crossed
Sanford Avenue."

I was quite impressed that Auntie drove a car; a woman driving was unheard of in Skopi. I soon realized, however, that she drove slowly, hesitantly. People honked at us all the way downtown. Some twenty minutes later—my nerves a little rattled—we pulled into a parking space outside Hudson's, Auntie's favorite department store.

I felt overwhelmed by both the gargantuan size of the store and the incredible quantity of merchandise for sale. Naturally, Auntie was quite familiar with the layout. She gave me a tour of the first floor. She rattled on and on—without taking a breath, it seemed. Given that I couldn't speak English, I just alternated between nodding and shaking my head. What a sight we must have been!

It was at Hudson's that I learned my first two English words, escalator and elevator. Auntie had to show me how to use them. We rode the escalator—which happily reminded me of a small rollercoaster I had ridden one summer at a fair in Tripoli—to the children's department on the second floor. She chose several dresses for me there, some of which I actually liked, and three pairs of shoes. While in the fitting room trying on my new clothes, Auntie made it clear that she intended to throw the black dress away right there in the store. I didn't mind that so much, but when she tried to do the same with my white sandals, I loudly objected. I still loved my sandals, which had taken my mother a few years to purchase for me. Auntie asked the sales clerk to put them in a bag, which I then carried around the store with me. The rest of the clothing, which now included shorts and a couple of shirts and several pieces of underwear, would be delivered, courtesy of Hudson's. My aunt didn't like carrying shopping bags around.

After our little shopping spree was over—which, I might add, my aunt thoroughly enjoyed—I followed her to a little soda shop on the third floor. We sat at the counter. Auntie ordered two hot fudge sundaes, a cup of coffee for herself and a glass of Coca-Cola for me.

The Sandals

I appreciated that my aunt had bought new clothes and shoes for me. I sure did need them. I didn't like the selections much is all. They were more my aunt's choices than mine. I especially disliked the red gingham dress. It hung loosely on my body and was a good two inches too long; plus, it came with a hideous, shiny plastic belt. As for the shoes she chose, they were big, boxy and tad too masculine for my taste. Still, my new acquisitions weren't black and I should have been grateful.

I was relieved not to have to wear black anymore. My father had been dead now for close to three years. Although I still missed him, the grieving period had passed. I wondered what my mother would have thought had she known that I had shed the black. I'm sure that she would have been happy for me. Thank God. I would have looked like Wednesday Addams of The Addams Family television show, wearing black clothes to school everyday.

We found Uncle Tom sitting on the porch swing when we got home. He was gently rocking to and fro while reading the Detroit News. Sitting there smoking his pipe and taking swigs from his customary bottle of Miller, he was the very picture of contentment. It was early evening with the sun about to set. A slight breeze fingered the wind chimes strung from the eaves. Uncle Tom had changed out of his work clothes. He lounged in a white undershirt, gray cotton trousers, and well worn brown leather slippers. This was the summer outfit he changed into once he got home from work.

Uncle Tom personified stability and well-being. Despite his imposing stature, he was warm, kind and accessible. I felt safe around him. Metaphorically speaking, he was like a big house in the middle of a snowstorm with a crackling fire in the fireplace. Auntie, on the other hand, made me feel tense and vulnerable. She was needy, high-strung, self-involved, and controlling. Her needs superseded mine—and everybody else's for that matter. I felt overshadowed in her presence. The fact that we weren't able to converse in the same language made things doubly hard.

Since I was pretty much overlooked by my family, I had developed a measure of independence and learned to take care of myself. Mostly left alone to fend for myself, certainly, not ideal, my childhood nevertheless, offered me the freedom to be myself, and forced me to use my wits for my survival. Auntie, on the other hand, treated me like a little kid who was clueless to my wants and needs. What came to mind was, "trust me, I know what is good for you."

While Auntie had difficulty perceiving me as a separate person, I did feel that she loved me. More loved, I thought, than even by my own family. She made me feel special, which was a new experience for me.

"We had a wonderful time shopping together, didn't we, Toula?" Auntie asked while recounting the day's events for Uncle Tom's benefit. "I bought Toula several beautiful dresses and some very nice shoes. They'll arrive in a couple of days. Toula will never have to wear black again. Isn't that wonderful, Tom? But she sure loves those sandals from the old country. She wouldn't part with them for the world."

She then hurried into the house to start dinner. I slumped beside Uncle Tom on the swing. "Now, what's the matter, Toulaki?" Uncle Tom looked at me worried.

I couldn't possibly tell him how I felt around Aunt Anna, so I lied and said, "I'm just tired."

"Hmmm?"

He gave me a squeeze and patted my head, then went back to reading the paper and puffing on his pipe. I sat there with Uncle Tom a while longer. My head felt like it weighed a ton. I attempted to make some sense of things, but I couldn't think clearly. Sadness was all I felt. Finally, I got up and ran upstairs to my bedroom. I looked around, and the strangeness of the room compounded my anguish. Numb, I fell on top of the bed while still clutching the shopping bag with my sandals inside. Memories of life back home with my family passed before my mind's eye. I was heart-sick. I cried from the depths of my soul.

After awhile, my cheeks stained with my tears, feeling completely exhausted, I opened my eyes and slowly sat up. I took the sandals out of the bag, and pressed them to my chest for a few minutes. I then searched for a special place in the closet to put them. I decided on the floor to the left of the door would be a good place for them. I kissed them as I would a friend and placed them in their special place. In the years to come, I'd look at them quite often, sometimes several times a day. The sandals took on a symbolic meaning for me. They represented a much-wanted gift from my mother and a reminder of my past. For the next seven years—that is, until I moved out—the sandals continued to be the link to my family and home. By then, the leather had become quite dry, and when I touched my beloved sandals, they cracked in several places, as my heart had so many times in the previous seven years.

An Unhappy Marriage

A s time went on, I began calling Aunt Anna Auntie. Though she
had been raised in privilege, most of her adult life she had to
work for a living. Even so, my aunt continued to live in the past. She
viewed most people as subjects who were there to meet her needs. She'd
walk into shops and restaurants, for example, and would stand by the door,
waiting to be served. I always found this quite embarrassing. I wanted to
tell my aunt that she lived in America, not in Europe. People didn't care
who you were, or who your family was, or how much money your family
had, or what social class you came from. But of course, I couldn't; she
would have been furious with me.

Auntie and Uncle Tom had been married for about thirty-five years
and had a very comfortable life. Uncle Tom retired with a very generous
pension at the age of sixty-two. My aunt had also recently retired from
her nursing career. But, hardly a year had gone by, when Uncle Tom went
back to work—this time at the University of Detroit—doing the same
kind of work he had done most of his life, stationery engineering. Perhaps
the lack of other interests coupled with a poor marriage prompted his
return to work. Fortunately for him, he enjoyed his work.

Although I had hoped that Uncle Tom and Auntie still loved each
other, what I saw transpire in the house told a different story. My aunt was
tense and unhappy. She had a lot of nervous energy, and always needed
to be busy. Her days were always full of some task or other, whether it be

shopping, visiting friends or cooking. Even in the evening after dinner, she would sit in her favorite chair and would rock back and forth, while knitting, crocheting, or doing needlepoint. She would occasionally glance at one of her favorite soap operas, or game shows on TV.

She was often critical of her husband, saying he was beneath her. When she got really angry at him, she'd call him *cafono,* which is Italian for peasant. I sensed that over the years there had been a lot of hurt feelings, which resulted in the two leading separate lives. They were obviously different. Not only did they come from different backgrounds, their personalities and temperament were different as well. My aunt's emotional neediness added to the mix.

They had grown apart. I sometimes wondered if there had been anything there to begin with. At a minimum, there must have been physical attraction between them, for they were both quite attractive, even in their sixties. I had seen photos of them as a young couple. They were really a quite stunning pair; they looked happy—well, at least in photographs.

Unlike his wife, Uncle Tom, was the retiring type. He had no problem relaxing in his favorite lounge chair, reading the paper, and puffing on his pipe. One would think that his presence would have had a calming affect on his wife, but it seemed to do just the opposite. Auntie seemed to be upset with Uncle Tom more often than not. Perhaps it upset her that he could be so content, when she herself couldn't. She was also angry that he had not lived up to her expectations. What were her expectations? I wasn't sure. She had regrets, resentments; she just couldn't come to terms with her life. So, she would stew in anger and then project that same anger into her environment, an environment that I unfortunately shared. I felt her sadness, her anger. But, it didn't appear to affect Uncle Tom; I guess he had learned, after many years, just to tune her out.

Uncle Tom had a simple lifestyle. Happy at work, he enjoyed doing little things around the house, like cutting the grass, pruning the trees, and detailing his car. He would enjoy one bottle of beer when he got home from work and one at dinner time. He kept up with current events by reading the newspaper and watching the evening news. He talked a little about his favorite Democrats, especially President Truman. He ended his evening by falling asleep on his favorite easy chair snoring contently; even the lamp light shining on his face didn't seem to bother him.

At around eleven o'clock every night, Auntie would call out to him, "Tom, Tom, you're snoring. Go to bed." He would briefly open his eyes and mumble incomprehensibly before falling back to sleep. At around eleven-thirty, after repeated reminders from his recalcitrant wife, Uncle Tom would finally get up and walk slowly upstairs to bed, where he would resume his snoring recital. Auntie would shake her head in exasperation.

Auntie was particularly unhappy that they had been unable to have children of their own. She would often mention this to me. One day, with sadness in her eyes, Auntie confided that when she was in her early twenties, she had become pregnant out of wedlock and had had an illegal abortion. She didn't say who performed the abortion, but the procedure had left her unable to bear children. She was devastated when she learned of this years later as she and Uncle Tom were trying to start a family. I never once heard Uncle Tom voice regret at not having children of their own, but it was very painful for my aunt.

"I will never, ever get over this. Having children is so important to me," Auntie would often tell me.

"Isn't there anything you can do, Auntie?" I would ask time and again.

"No, I have checked with many doctors. The damage is done."

She hadn't—couldn't possibly—tell Uncle Tom about the abortion. She felt guilty about it herself and believed—rightly or wrongly—that Uncle Tom would judge her harshly if he ever found out. I didn't agree with her conclusion, but she couldn't bring herself to tell her husband, so she talked to me instead.

Thus I became Auntie's confidante and companion. She took me with her every place she went. We visited her friends, shopped, went to the movies and out to dinner together. She confided in me as she would a friend. I felt overwhelmed and resentful. I wanted my own life. I was afraid to let her know how I felt for I was certain she would get angry and not speak to me for several days, as she had done more than once in the past.

Uncle Tom generally resisted Auntie's invitations to join her when she visited friends. He would also beg off when she suggested they go out to dinner, to the movies, or to the opera together. She finally gave up asking altogether, but felt a great deal of resentment toward him as a result.

Besides attending a couple of summer festivals sponsored by the Greek Orthodox Church, the one thing Uncle Tom was willing to do with his wife was to have dinner at The Greek Taverna on Monroe Street in Greek Town. I would usually order *augolemono,* a tangy egg-lemon soup, Greek salad with feta cheese and Kalamata olives, and, of course, roasted leg of lamb and potatoes. I would have baked custard pudding— *galatoboureko*—for dessert. This was a lot of food for a little kid, but I just couldn't resist stuffing my mouth.

One night at the Taverna not long after I arrived from Greece, I noticed that Uncle Tom had left lot of money on the table. Being a conscientious little kid, I scooped up the money and, handing it to him, said, "Uncle Tom you forgot this money on the table. Here, take it." Uncle Tom giggled. He took the money from my hand and placed it back on the table explaining, "This is a tip for the waiter for having served us."

"Really?" I said. That struck me as a very nice thing to do. Had my mother ever tipped the servers in Greece? I don't recall ever seeing any money left on the table the few times we had gone out to eat. But then, we would always have our meals in the underground, inexpensive, restaurants.

We would walk down a flight of stairs and go directly to the kitchen. We'd point out what we wanted, and then we'd carry our food to the table; no need for waiters.

"*Yiasas pethia, te magerepsate simera?*" Mother would greet the cooks, asking what they had cooked that day.

"*Oti thelete ta exoume, kiria mou*"—whatever you want, we have it madam—they'd respond enthusiastically.

We would also attend a Greek festival or two during the summer. Greeks and non-Greeks would attend these festivals held at public parks. There would be delicious Greek food, pastries, drinks and live Greek music. I sure enjoyed the music; it reminded me of home. The bouzouki, an instrument similar to a mandolin, featured prominently in most of the traditional songs they played. The clarinet, guitar, and sometimes the violin and drums complemented the bouzouki. I enjoyed dancing, but often I was too shy to get on the dance floor.

"Go ahead Toula, dance, dance, have a good time," Auntie would encourage me. Finally, getting the courage up to join others in the circle dance, I found myself dancing for quite awhile, even sometimes taking the lead. The festivals were a lot of fun. We thoroughly enjoyed them. Unfortunately, Uncle Tom did not want to do anything else with his wife.

My aunt, personally, however, had a number of positive attributes. She was social and enjoyed friends and entertaining. She loved the opera, symphony and the ballet. She loved to travel. She was quite creative and had an eye for esthetics; she had created a lovely, comfortable home with a sense of style and furnishings of high quality. She loved food and was a gourmet cook. She especially loved spaghetti. We had spaghetti and meatballs three times a week. Auntie would start cooking soon after she finished her morning pot of coffee.

"See, Toula, this is the best way to make delicious spaghetti sauce," she would say. "Cook it slowly on low heat, while adding small amounts of water throughout the day. It will bring out the wonderful, rich flavor in the sauce. Then, about two hours before dinner, mix the ground meat—always beef—with an egg, onions, garlic, oregano, sweet basil, marjoram and thyme. Then, roll each meatball the size of a large round plum, and drop each one carefully in the meat sauce. It's very important that the meatballs cook in the sauce. Never fry them because they'll become tough, and then you'll have ruined the whole meal."

I learned to love spaghetti—perhaps not as much as my aunt did—but I loved the days when Auntie cooked the sauce. The aroma from the sauce would waft throughout the house, while Enrico Caruso, Auntie's favorite tenor, played on the phonograph. I could see how much my aunt enjoyed all of this by the look in her eyes. She was totally absorbed in the magic of it all. It was during these times that I saw her relax. I even noticed a little dance that she would do. Her body would sway from side to side, her hands affecting motion in the air. It seemed Auntie was dancing with an imaginary lover. She would sip a little sherry, as well, enhancing the whole experience. Her spirits were definitely high during these times; she was in her element. No doubt, my aunt had passion and tried to live life to the fullest.

Just watching my aunt eat, for example. She held the fork in her left hand, knife in the right, gently placing the food in her mouth. She used a soup spoon to help roll the spaghetti around her fork. "Never cut the spaghetti," she'd say. "You would be breaking a major etiquette rule. Simply turn the spoon around and around, until the spaghetti is wrapped around the fork."

Auntie would demonstrate the proper form, lightly smacking her lips, and dabbing at the corners of her mouth with a cloth napkin before each forkful. This was followed with a generous sip of wine. After dinner, she would take a deep drag from her Chesterfield, blowing smoke through her nostrils or out of her moth with a sigh of deep satisfaction. She would watch the smoke form curlicues in the air.

Auntie also gave small dinner parties on a regular basis. The guest list almost always included her nephew John and his wife Mary, her adult foster daughter Carol and family, and a friend or two. My job on those occasions was to set the table; Auntie had taught me where each plate, glass, eating utensil would go. I enjoyed these get-togethers a great deal.

I had warm friendships with John and his wife Mary. Mary was a voracious reader, always bringing a book along.

"What are you reading now Mary?" I'd ask.

In no time, she'd take her book out of her purse and tell me what it was about. She would often promise to pass on the book to me to read—once she finished—and she usually did. I especially liked reading her mystery novels.

Carol, Harold, and their two daughters were friendly enough, but not very expressive; they were reserved and extremely polite. Although we didn't interact much, I liked them a lot. They had a nice, positive presence. They were all blond with blue eyes and a slight build, with the exception of Harold who carried a few extra pounds. I often wondered how Carol had coped with Auntie, whom she called Anna. I had hoped that she and I might have a chance to talk privately one day—I figured she might be able to give me some pointers—but, alas, that day never came.

Carol seemed to be a matter-of-fact person. I only knew that Carol's mother had died when she was about six or seven years old. Her father could not care for her and placed her in foster care. I believe he had remarried and his wife didn't want to care for Carol. When she was around seven years old and after having already been in two foster homes, she came to live with Auntie and Uncle Tom. She stayed until she got married at the age of twenty-four. Somehow Carol managed well under Auntie's care, for she seemed well adjusted. I can't say, however, that I ever saw much love pass between them. Even her relationship with Uncle Tom struck me as rather cool. It was hard to tell with Carol in any case as she was so reserved.

Auntie and I canned fruit, vegetables, jams and jellies every summer. For a couple of weeks, usually in July, the kitchen would be at full speed, running like a well-oiled machine. Auntie and I metamorphosed into busy little bees, trying to juggle a number of things all at once. Those two weeks were always full of fun and excitement.

We started by checking the crates of fresh vegetables and fruit that Uncle Tom had brought home the night before; he had bought them directly from a farmer at a produce stand. We would lift the crates onto the kitchen table for a closer look. We carefully examined the string beans, cauliflower, tomatoes, apricots, pears, peaches, cherries, small cucumbers for pickling, and brightly colored berries. Anything that didn't meet my Aunt's standards was discarded. No blemished or bruised fruit was acceptable. She would toss fruit if it was either too ripe or not ripe enough. Having washed the fruit and vegetables in warm water, we would carefully placed them in large aluminum pots and covered them with water. A separate pot was used to sterilize large glass mason jars and their lids. Once we had turned the stove on, it pretty much stayed on for the next couple of weeks.

When we heard the liquid bubbling inside the pots, we would lift the lids and peek inside; the vividly colored vegetables and fruit would be dancing to the beat of the boiling juice. We watched as the escaping steam created small clouds on the ceiling; moisture clung to the walls and windows. We inhaled the appetizing fumes till our lungs were full.

We covered the kitchen table with newspaper and tools of the trade: large spoons, forks, ladles, prongs, and bowls. The sterilized mason jars, now on the table, would be filled with the glorious food. We checked the cooking vegetables and fruit, adjusted the heat accordingly, and kept an eye on the clock. When it was time, we'd turn the gas burners off, and, using large potholders, we took the pots to the sink. We carefully poured some of the juice into large plastic containers, and spooned the fruit and vegetables into the jars. We filled the jars three quarters full with the scalded produce, and then topped them with the beautifully colored liquid. Loosely tightening the lids, we then left this incredible assortment of food art sit on the table for several days. The display reminded me of a painting. I found it visually pleasing, not to mention mouth-watering.

Not only was the house suffused with the wonderful aromas, so was the immediate neighborhood. The sweet smell of raspberry and wild berry jellies and jams, the sweet and tangy smell of peaches, apricots and cherries—all our senses were awakened to this incredibly appetizing scent.

After a few days, we tighten the lids, labeled and dated each jar, and stored them all in a dark room in the basement. We carefully placed each jar in a row, depending on its contents; vegetables in one row, fruit in another, and jam and jellies in yet another. Before closing the door and going back upstairs, I waived goodbye to my "special friends." Throughout the year, the food was served for breakfast, lunch, dinner and even dessert. My aunt also gave her creation as gifts to family, friends and neighbors.

I was her right hand assistant, as it were. She taught me every aspect of the canning process and, to my surprise, she gave me free reign—well, within reason. She enjoyed what she was doing so much that it rubbed off on me. I very much relished being part of this project. Creating something as wonderful as this and juggling so many balls at the same time was an exciting and fun time for me.

Auntie had a number of women friends, and we would visit them quite often. She was eager to introduce me to everyone she knew. The experience was not much fun for me, but I knew I had no choice but to go along. She would say, "Today, we will visit another *felenada*," female friend in Greek. Usually, after introductions, the friends would talk in English while I sat around. This didn't seem to bother my aunt much—or her friends, for that matter. I could, of course, have stayed home, but that wasn't an option.

As I tried hard to assert myself, tried to create a life for myself—to no avail—my resentment of Auntie grew. She had all the power—and was too emotionally needy—to recognize my needs. I tried a few times to enlist Uncle Tom's help; for him to intervene on my behalf. But, he resisted—and when I pushed a little—he said, "She's your aunt. She means well. She loves you, Toula. Do as she says."

I was shocked at first to hear this, but, in retrospect, I understood his position. She was his wife after all, and he probably felt helpless around the situation. This greatly upset me at that time, however. I became angry with Uncle Tom, and lost a little respect for him too. Eventually, though, I forgave him. Who knows—perhaps my aunt's anger toward her husband might have been of a similar nature. She might have been angry at him for giving up and withdrawing and not really being there for her. It is hard to speculate, but that's how it was, and it remained so all the while I lived with them.

Adapting

Another of Auntie's projects was teaching me English. Unbeknownst to me at that time, however, was that she spoke English poorly herself—and with an Italian accent to boot. Here are some choice examples: *Sardy* meant Saturday, *crema*—cream. When she wanted a hamburger, she would ask for a *hamborgor*, and when she was thirsty, she'd ask for *CoocooCola*. Obviously, my English lessons left a lot to be desired.

But, they did take place. Each evening after dinner for one hour the family room was transformed into an English classroom. Auntie would sit in her favorite red chair. Next to her chair, a portable TV tray served as a small writing desk where Auntie placed the tools of her trade—namely, a notebook, pencil and pen. Nearby was a matching ottoman, which served as my seat.

"Toula, move closer. Be careful now, move the ottoman just at my feet, don't hurt my feet now," she would say. So I would move the ottoman closer, making sure not to touch her feet. "Now, go to the bookcase," she would say, pointing at the opposite wall, "and bring that large, red rimmed dictionary to me."

The lesson would begin once I sat back down. She would place the dictionary on her lap, referring to it throughout the lesson. We would start with the alphabet. She would pronounce each letter first—Italian accent and all—and I would repeat after her.

"Say A-a-a-h, just like me. Watch the way I move my tongue now."

She opened her mouth as wide as she could in order to demonstrate proper tongue placement. I always thought that my aunt's tongue was a little redder than normal, which always drove me to distraction. She would write each letter in her notebook in both upper and lowercase letters. Handing me the notebook and pen, she would tell me to copy the alphabet on the lines just below hers. I have to admit that Auntie's printing was very good, especially compared to mine. She insisted that I pronounce each letter as I copied it. I did this over and over till I sounded just like an old Italian *yenta*. Auntie never forgot to convene class—on weeknights, that is; thankfully, I had weekends off.

Still, I have to give Auntie credit. She tried. Unfortunately, she just didn't have sufficient command of the English language herself to teach me properly. So, I spoke English as badly as she did, that is, until I started going to school—where I was exposed to teachers and native-born speakers—that my English started to improve. I didn't truly begin to speak English well, however, until I was thirty years old, when I married my American-born, college educated second husband.

I was ambivalent about learning English, in any case. Since I believed that I'd find a way to get back to Greece, learning English didn't make a whole lot of sense to me. I did appreciate that my aunt took the time to teach me, however, so I responded by being receptive to her lessons. But, it was beyond frustrating having Auntie as the teacher. I used to wish that I had a real teacher, like Miss Petropoulou back in Skopi.

I would often think of my beloved teacher, and how fun her teaching was. Not only did she teach the core curriculum in fun and interesting ways, but she taught us music as well. I especially liked the classroom sing-a-along. I can still remember the words to *Gerakina,* one of the most popular songs of the day: *kinise e gerakina sto pigathe na pai na fere nero.*

The title character *Gerakina* was a free spirited young woman.

Immodestly dressed, she would flirt with boys while walking to the well to fetch water. She didn't care what anyone thought of her. I wish I could be as free as *Gerakina*.

Miss Petropoulou also served as a role model for me. She brought style to our little backward town. She dressed beautifully—crisp white blouse and navy blue skirt—a look she accessorized with fun jewelry. She wore red lipstick, and matching rouge. She parted her silky black hair on the left, and let it hang loosely to her shoulders. I especially admired an ebony clip she'd sometimes wear. Each morning when I got up and started to get ready for school, I'd think of my beautiful teacher and how I could make myself look more like her—not an easy feat.

I had been gone from my home for over one month now, and still had not received a single letter from my family. I had written a number of letters to them—several while en route to America—since my arrival. But, they hadn't written back. This made me miss them even more. As days went by without correspondence, I began to worry that something had happened to them. This only compounded my loneliness, my sadness. I expressed my concern to Uncle Tom, but each time he assured me with his usual gentle patting on the head and calming voice. "Not to worry Toulaki; any day now the postman will deliver the letter you have been waiting for." He'd then go right back to reading his newspaper and puffing on his pipe.

The little pep talk managed to console me for all of a few minutes. Every day I waited for the postman, but no letter would arrive. Eventually, I'd find myself sitting outside on the front steps waiting for Joe, the postman; by now, we had become quite friendly. He would acknowledge me with a smile before sifting through the bundle of letters in his hands in search of a letter with my name on it. But time and again, with a sad look in his eyes he would shake his head no. I'd wake up each morning hoping that this was the day I'd receive my long-awaited letter, but each day my hopes would be dashed.

What's wrong with them? I wondered. "Have they forgotten me already?" I would sometimes say aloud, feeling heartsick. As there were no phones in Skopi, letter writing was the standard means of communication. Even though I kept telling myself that it could take several days—or even weeks—for a letter from Greece to reach me in Detroit, this reasoning offered little consolation. My aunt—seeing how sad I became after the postman came and went without a letter for me—would urge me to visit the Greek family down the street.

"Go see the Panagiotis family, Toula. I'm sure they'll be happy to see you."

"Okay," I'd say, nodding my head sadly.

Actually, the Panagiotises were not Greek at all. They were Turkish. Having lived in Greece for a number of years before emigrating, they had assimilated the Greek culture; they even attended orthodox service at Hagia Sofia in Greek Town. I visited them quite often, and found the experience rather pleasant. I enjoyed being able to speak Greek again, and if I were lucky, they'd serve Greek food. I became close with the two girls, Patty and Sophia; they were a few years older than me. They were both tall, rather attractive girls with olive complexion and black hair. I, on the other hand, had a delicate build, weighing less than a hundred pounds and was around five feet tall at that time. Despite being overshadowed by the girls, I enjoyed spending time with them. We would often be out walking either to the corner variety store to buy makeup and candy, or to the movies. We sometimes drove to the beach, where we spent afternoons sunbathing and swimming. They were nice enough companions, but, other than our shared heritage, we were really quite different. I knew, though, that I needed friends, so I kept in touch.

Their brother Jordan was closest to my age. He was stocky, carrying an extra twenty to twenty-five pounds, but a sweet kid who obviously loved food. In summer, he would shave off all of his curly black hair. He'd usually wear a t-shirt, shorts and sandals. He seemed to spend a lot of time in his own little world. He didn't interact very much, probably because no one bothered to talk to him, except, that is, to give him orders.

"Do this Jordan. Bring that to me, Jordan. Don't eat so much, Jordan. You're fat enough as it is, Jordan!"

His sisters didn't pay much attention to him. I could see he felt left out. I knew the feeling well, for I felt the same way when I was growing up with my three older brothers. I empathized with him. Unlike me though, always fighting to stay in the loop, it seemed Jordan had become resigned to being alone in a house full of women. With his sad, dark eyes, he would aimlessly look for food, opening the refrigerator and cupboards, or would grab a fruit from the fruit bowl. Food had become his friend, it seemed.

He would entertain himself watching television, listing to records, dealing solitaire, and playing basketball by himself. I felt a little sorry for him. I wanted to befriend him, but, not knowing how or whether it was even appropriate. I'm sure as he grows up he'll make friends and be happy, I assured myself.

I frankly found the Panagiotises odd. They didn't talk so much as yell. They spoke as though they had pebbles in their mouths. They spoke over one another, admittedly in a good-natured sort of way. The home atmosphere was chaotic. At times they spoke Arabic, and sometimes a mix of Arabic and Greek. They reminded me more than a little of the gypsies who would come to Skopi and camp out for the summer; they even resembled them. Despite this ambivalence, I was grateful to have people who spoke Greek living nearby.

The Pintos' lived across the street from the Panagiotises in a little blue house with white trim. Louis Pinto was first generation Sicilian-American.

He must have been around fifty at the time. He was married to Sharon whom the Panagiotises referred to as a WASP. They had two teenage daughters. The younger of the two, Darlene, was my age. We soon became fast friends. She was short and stocky—but very cute. She wore her black hair short. She applied hair gel that added shine and made her hair stand straight up. She wore mostly t-shirts and shorts. She looked and acted like a tomboy. A matter-of-fact kind of a girl, who wore no makeup, came straight to the point, and didn't seem to have much patience. I identified with her, for I too thought of myself as a tomboy. Her fifteen-year-old sister Geraldine, on the other hand, was quite feminine, with a slight build and long brown hair. Plus, she was a bit of a flirt.

Darlene and I spent a lot of time together at each other's homes, doing normal kid stuff. We restyled each other's hair, and tried wearing makeup; everything from lipstick, blush, to eyeliner, mascara, and even curled our eyelashes. But we decided we weren't ready for grown up stuff. We would often do our homework together. I was good at math and Darlene in English, so we would help each other out.

I knew Darlene was a genuinely good person despite sometimes being aloof. I thought I sensed sadness, not that she ever said anything. It was rumored that her father was an alcoholic and worked sporadically. Her mother—whom I rarely saw—had to work to make ends meet. Darlene never spoke of her family. She walked around smiling as if everything was fine at home. I never pressed her on the matter.

I would join the Pintos for car rides in the country practically every Sunday afternoon after they came home from church. Darlene was always welcome at our house. Auntie would take us out to Metropolitan Beach, a brand new beach with miles of soft, warm sand, about a half hour's drive from home. My aunt would place her umbrella and folding chair some distance from us, settling down with a book, while Darlene and I, in our one piece bathing suits would find a place near the water's edge. We would dash in and out of the surf giggling, splashing one another, swimming and sunbathing. Sometimes we would bury each other in the sand, leaving only our heads above ground, our eyes looking up at the golden sun as it slowly set. When a slight breeze picked up, that would be our signal to pack up and head for home. Darlene would also come along on weekends, when we went to our summer home at Lake Huron. Eventually, I would spend more time with Darlene than with the Panagiotises.

Days, then weeks passed without word from my family. I still held out hope that I would be going back home soon. While I was planning on returning home, Auntie and Uncle Tom were talking about enrolling me in school in September. There was an elementary school just a few miles away. My aunt wasn't sure I would be able to attend a regular public school on account of my limited English; there was a chance I would have to go to a school for the non-native students instead.

A few weeks before the start of the new school year, Auntie and I prepared for a meeting with Mr. Anderson, principal of Wilkins Elementary School.

"Toula, please put on your best dress; you know, that red and white checked dress that I like so much. We are going to visit Mr. Anderson today."

As usual, I did as told. She also put her best dress on, too, the beige knit one with the matching bag. She pulled on her white gloves, grabbed her bag and car keys, and off we went to meet with Mr. Anderson.

Wilkins Elementary School consisted of a large, two-story brick building and a large playground. A chain link fence ran around the perimeter of the school. Students entered the building through tall, arched double doors. Once inside, corridors led to a spacious lobby with high ceilings, and a number of arched windows. There were lockers on both sides of the corridor. Stairs with a bronze handrail led to the second floor. This was very different indeed from my two-room schoolhouse in Skopi.

"I'm Anna Siakotos. This is my niece, Toula. We have an appointment with Principal Anderson."

"How do you do," responded the school secretary.

"Fine, I'm sure," my aunt answered.

The secretary smiled at me. I returned the smile.

"Please, sit down. Mr. Anderson will be right with you."

She went back to her paperwork. We sat on a wooden bench across from her.

Mr. Anderson appeared a few minutes later. An attractive man in his early fifties, he was dressed in a gray suit, white shirt and navy blue tie.

"Mrs. Siakotos, I'm Mr. Anderson." They shook hands. He then looked at me.

"This must be your niece Toula."

"How do you do, Mr. Anderson? Thank you for seeing us. Yes, this is my niece, Toula."

He nodded and smiled. He opened the door to his office and invited us in, closing the door behind us.

"Please, sit down."

Mr. Anderson pointed to a couple of chairs in front of his desk. Auntie started to explain while I glanced around the room. Mr. Anderson's office was quite spacious and comfortable. There were two large picture windows facing the front yard of the building. The trees outside swayed slightly in the breeze, brushing against the window pain. From where he sat, Mr. Anderson could watch the students outside. The walls of his office were decorated with a variety of framed diplomas and degrees. A large framed landscape painting hung on the wall behind his desk. A rhododendron in a clay pot appeared to have been there for quite a few years. The plant had grown considerably, covering the walls, nearly halfway to the ceiling. A bunch of strings held this gigantic plant in place. But the poor plant needed even more help as its branches hung in all directions. There were two framed photos on his desk; I figured they were of his family. Black, plastic trays stacked three high, were filled with paperwork, while a small stack was neatly placed in front of him.

"My niece speaks very little English, having recently arrived from Greece," I heard my aunt say.

"Hmm, hmm, I see," responded Mr. Anderson.

"We wonder whether Toula could attend your school. It would be so convenient, as the school is only a few miles from our home."

"Hmm, hmm, let me see now."

He looked at me as one might an object in a bazaar. It reminded me of the buyers in Skopi trying to decide whether they wanted to buy my family's produce. *Will I be getting my money's worth,* they pondered silently. He spoke to me briefly, and, much to my surprise, I understood what he said. Moreover, not only did I understand him, but I was able to respond. For some reason, I can't remember exactly what he said, but I do know he understood whatever it is I said in return. Apparently, Auntie's English lessons had worked, after all. Our little exchange was apparently sufficient proof for Mr. Anderson.

"Yes, yes, it might be a little difficult for Toula at the beginning, but she'll do just fine. I can see, that she's a smart little girl. I like to welcome you both to Wilkins Elementary School. Remember to fill out the paperwork with the secretary on your way out."

Auntie was delighted—not to mention relieved—that I would be going to Wilkins Elementary, its being so close to home and all.

"Thank you, Mr. Anderson," she said, getting up.

He showed us out. Auntie squeezed my hand, excitedly. I frankly didn't know what to think. I figured that if my aunt thought it a good idea, it was okay by me. We strode out of the principal's office triumphant. Auntie completed the paperwork with the secretary's assistance, and then we happily left the school building.

I checked out the playground as we walked out the front door. It had a baseball diamond. I could see a large group of kids playing out there;

I could picture myself among them. *I guess this is it*, I thought, realizing that I would be back here again, in the not too distant future. *But, what about returning to Greece?* I asked myself. Incredibly, that didn't seem so important anymore. How strange!

I thought instead about attending school—this school, Wilkins Elementary—in less than a month's time. I was pleasantly surprised that I had mostly understood the discussion in Mr. Anderson's office. I hoped that I would manage my school work just as well.

Instead of going home, we took a detour to Sander's Confectionary Shop, where we had our regular hot-fudge sundaes. This was a time for celebration, and Auntie and I celebrated with our favorite dessert. As usual, she ordered for the both of us while I grabbed the small spoon the waitress placed in front of me. I couldn't wait to dig into the warm hot-fudge and cold vanilla ice cream. We finished our dessert in no time flat and rushed back to our car. It was getting late and Auntie fretted about getting dinner ready on time.

I was all excited to get home and run across the street to talk with my friend Darlene. My aunt had barely parked the car when I asked if I could go across the street to see her.

"Okay, but be sure to be home for dinner. We have good news for your uncle, not to mention the delicious dinner I'll have prepared." "I promise," I said, rushing off.

I found Darlene—for the first time—looking distracted and unhappy.

"Hi, what's wrong?"

"Nothing," she said, "Let's go outside."

"Is it your Dad, Darlene?"

"Yeah," she admitted.

"I'm sorry."

"Yeah, me too."

I waited patiently for her to elaborate, but she just didn't seem to want to talk.

"So, what's up?" she asked in an offhand way.

"Darlene, you wouldn't believe this, but I'll be going to the same school as you in September. Principal Anderson said I could."

"Great, great, Toula," she said absent-mindedly, "We'll take the bus together."

I could see Darlene was preoccupied and not in the mood to talk, so we said goodbye. I was concerned about her, but not knowing what else to do, I slowly walked home, my excitement diminished.

My aunt was in the kitchen preparing dinner when I walked in. I set the table without being asked. Then I checked if the mailman had come.

"Yes, he has, but there's no letter for you. I'm sorry, Toula." She looked at me sadly.

I ran upstairs to my room and wrote another letter. Tears stained the paper on which I wrote:

> *I miss you all very much. Have you all forgotten me already? Please, please, write to me. I love you all so much.*
>
> *Your daughter and sister,*
> *Toula*

The Cottage

M y aunt and uncle's summer home was called The Cottage. It was located at Lake Huron about sixty-five miles north of Detroit.

We spent pretty much every weekend at The Cottage when school was out in summer. Auntie and I would usually drive there on Friday morning. Uncle Tom would join us after he got off work that evening.

"Toula, bring up the two suitcases and a couple of boxes from the basement—and hurry; we are already running late. By the time we pack, it'll be close to noon, and you know it takes over an hour to get there— that is, if we're lucky and don't run into traffic."

"Okay, okay," I'd say, gulping down my frosted flakes and rushing down to the basement. Reaching the bottom step, I would make a quick u-turn and grab my aunt's large, navy blue Simmons, and my smaller, non-descript, brown leather bag from underneath the staircase. I would make a second trip for the cardboard boxes that Uncle Tom kept beside the suitcases.

Auntie was already busy packing in her bedroom upstairs. She took several items of clothing from the closets and bureau drawers and placed them on top of her bed. After selecting a couple of sun dresses and a sun bonnet for herself, she went into my bedroom and picked out several shorts and tops for me. She also made sure to bring a couple of nightgowns, several pairs of underwear, my black bathing suit, a couple of tubes of suntan lotion and sundry toiletries.

In the cardboard boxes we packed clean linen, including several warm blankets, pillows, and a couple of afghans that my aunt had knitted. We filled grocery bags with enough food to last the weekend: milk, eggs, bacon, coffee, sugar, flour, pancake mix, ground meat for hamburgers, hot dogs, potato salad, pickles, mayonnaise, mustard and ketchup, bananas, apples, watermelon, bread and hamburger buns.

"I think we have enough food, don't you Toula? I'm sure Tom will bring more—you know, the things that he likes, like some Miller beer, probably a couple of t-bone steaks, Coke, and tootsie rolls for you. He thinks you love tootsie rolls, did you know that?"

"I don't really like tootsie rolls all that much—they are too sweet and sticky—but somehow Uncle Tom has got in his head that I love them. He even calls me tootsie, sometimes! I bet he likes the candy more than I do, don't you think Auntie?"

"I think you are probably right about that."

We looked around to make sure we weren't forgetting anything.

"Well, I think we got everything. Let's hope we can fit it all in the car," Auntie said.

We managed to load the large boxes and suitcases into the trunk. The bags went onto the floorboards in the back of the car. I pulled one of the afghans from the bag and threw it across the backseat, knowing that before we reached the cottage I would take a little nap, and would need the afghan.

My aunt was anxious to get going. It was a beautiful sunny day, and to our relief, there was very little traffic on the road. I was not the best traveling companion. The motion of the car would lull me to quietness and then to sleep, which frustrated my aunt to no end, for she loved to talk. Hardly a half hour had passed before I found myself climbing into the backseat for my little nap.

"Toula, wake up, wake up. We've arrived." I rubbed my eyes open and threw off the afghan. Auntie opened the car door. "Get up sleepy head, we're here."

I looked out the car window. The grass had grown tall, the bushes had gotten taller and wider. Flowers bloomed everywhere. Birds and butterflies buzzed about. Still, The Cottage looked kind of forlorn to me. It had been there all by its lonesome for nearly three quarters of the year, waiting to be inhabited by its family again, or so I fancied.

I got out of the car and stretched my arms. Squinting from the bright sun, I took in the glory of the countryside: the crisp, fresh air, the fragrant flowers, the chirping birds, the ants crawling up my legs, the mosquitoes buzzing around my head. Then, Auntie's voice rudely broke the spell nature had cast.

"Come on now. No time to dally. We have a lot of work to do."

As usual, Auntie could not really appreciate this incredible setting—no, not until all the work was done. *Work before pleasure* was her motto.

"The Cottage has been closed all winter; it needs to be aired out," she said.

Having found the keys in her bag, she opened the front door. We walked inside.

"Let's open all the doors and windows and let the sun in. Sure is musty!"

The Cottage, designed by my aunt, sat on a five-acre parcel of land. Along with tall pine and oak trees, the property was also covered in native bushes and plants like scotch broom, wild heck weed and common ninebark. Auntie and Uncle Tom had added additional plants over the years—replanting each year—including marigolds, geraniums, and gladiolus. Climbing rose bushes framed the front door. Auntie had planted rose bushes all over the property as they were her favorite flower. The air smelled of rose perfume. We would fill every vase in the house with red, yellow and white roses. Snapdragons and hydrangeas, tulips and iris were in abundance, too. There was an apple and a plum tree. I would get sick to my stomach from eating too many sour green apples.

With the exception of a small area in front of the house where Uncle Tom had planted grass, the rest of the property was left as nature had intended. Uncle Tom wielded a mighty weed whacker against the tall weeds. He used large clippers to trim the bushes and trees. I would often follow him around, sometimes stopping to cut a flower and smell its sweet scent. When Uncle Tom got tired, he would stop and sit a while, wiping his sweaty brow with a handkerchief that he kept in his back pocket. I would hand him his Miller beer.

The Cottage consisted of a spacious living room with a large stone fireplace, an airy kitchen, three bedrooms and a bathroom—all on one floor. There was also a utility room where we kept the icebox, a pantry, and a linen closet. The bottom part of the exterior wall was made of stone. Auntie and I thought it lent the house character. Auntie, Uncle Tom and the three foster children living with them at that time had hand-picked the stones from the shores of Lake Huron. They carted them by wheelbarrow back to the construction site.

Auntie and Uncle Tom would enjoy their morning coffee inside the large enclosed porch, while I sipped on hot chocolate. We would sit in this spacious room watching nature in action. Sparrows, humming birds, ravens, and the occasional crow would fly by. I especially liked watching the amber-colored butterflies flutter from one flower to another, competing with bees for sweet nectar.

"But we have work to do now," my aunt reminded me.

We went through the whole house opening all the windows and doors.

"Toula, turn all the faucets on, and let the water run till its clear."

I went into the kitchen, turned the faucet on, and watched brown water gush out of the tap.

"Yuk!"

"What's wrong?" Auntie called out from the next room.

"The water, it's brown!"

"It'll clear up in no time; you'll see. The water has been sitting in the pipes all winter."

When I turned the faucet on in the bathroom, brown water sputtered out there too.

After a couple of minutes, however, the water began to run clear just like Auntie said. I stuck a finger under the tap. The water was so cold that I thought my finger would fall off.

"Okay, Auntie, what's next?"

"Let's bring everything in from the car."

We brought in the suitcases inside and put them in the bedrooms. We placed the boxes on the kitchen floor. We then made the beds with flannel sheets and matching pillowcases. We covered the beds with quilts Auntie had made. We swept the floors, and vacuumed the carpets. We swept away the cobwebs from the walls and ceiling.

"Auntie," I asked, pointing at a cobweb tucked snuggly in a corner. "Could you please get that one there, the one in the corner?"

She took the broom from my hand and tried sweeping the web away, over and over, till, exasperated, she said, "We'll give this little job to your uncle when he arrives later; it's just too high for me."

"Okay," I said taking the broom back, and sweeping around the front door.

"Should we turn the sprinklers on, or just wait for Uncle Tom to do that, too?" I asked, having noticed that the grass had begun to turn brown.

"No, that's another of your uncle's jobs around here, and, anyway, it's such a pain dragging the hoses and sprinklers out. I wouldn't know where to put them."

Among his many other duties around the house, Uncle Tom would make sure that we had enough propane for heating and cooking. He would go into town to place an order when we ran low. He would also buy blocks of ice for the icebox while there.

We worked non-stop for about three hours. The sun was setting. Evening approached. Since the house was still quite cold, Auntie turned on the thermostat. Nothing happened.

"Either the pilot's off, or we need propane. We have to wait for your uncle to arrive to figure that out. Let's take the groceries out of the bags, and put the food away."

Looking at the ground meat and hotdogs, Auntie wondered aloud, "I hope the meat doesn't spoil." She looked for the coldest place in the house to store it. Handling the food must have triggered hunger pangs in my aunt for she said, "I'm hungry," as she dug into the grocery bags.

"Do you want something to eat, Toula?"

"Now that you mention it . . ."

In a hurry to get to The Cottage, we had skipped lunch. Now we were famished. We pulled out a loaf of Wonder bread, and packages of bologna and sliced American cheese. We spread mayonnaise on the bread slices, and piled on the bologna and cheese. Auntie cut the sandwiches diagonally.

"That should hold us until Uncle Tom arrives. We will have a nice dinner, either here at The Cottage or at a nearby restaurant," Auntie said.

I strolled through the house while munching on my sandwich. It felt a little strange the first day, as if we were chasing out ghosts or something that had occupied the house in our absence. The bedrooms, unlike the shared common rooms, still felt cold and uninviting. *It'll feel better, be patient*, I assured myself, *before the weekend is over—and much, much better on weekends to follow.* Keeping that in mind, I placed all my toiletries in the bathroom, took out my nightgown and placed it on top of my bed, and hung my few items of clothing in the closet. Just as the sun was about to set, I heard my uncle's Packard pulling up outside. I ran out to greet him with Auntie right behind me.

"Tom, we need propane, and ice for the icebox, I'm afraid the hamburger meat might spoil. And another thing, the heat would not go on when I turned the thermostat up."

Uncle Tom shook his head as he got out of the car. I felt a little sorry for him, knowing that he had worked all day, and then the long drive to The Cottage. *Poor Uncle Tom,* I thought, reaching for his hand, partly to comfort him and partly because I was happy to see him. He took my hand, and then bent down and picked me up. He held me in his arms for a couple of minutes.

"Toulaki, you want to go into town with me? We need to order ice and propane."

"Sure, Uncle Tom," I said gladly.

"Auntie, do you need anything?" Uncle Tom asked.

Thinking for a second, she then said, "Nope. I don't think so."

I sat on the passenger seat next to Uncle Tom. The Packard smelled of his favorite pipe tobacco, sweet and spicy.

"How long did it take you to drive here, Uncle Tom?" I asked.

"Oh, I don't know, couple of hours I guess."

"Oh, you must have run into traffic?"

"That I did, sweetheart."

He looked at me sweetly, giving me his usual pat on the head. It took all of five minutes to drive into town. Uncle Tom pulled into a parking space outside of Jack's Hardware Store, and shut off the engine. He slowly pulled himself out of the car, while holding to the steering wheel with his right hand. I could see that Uncle Tom was tired; his pace was much slower than usual.

"Hi, fellas," Uncle Tom greeted the two men standing behind the counter. Jack and Ron had been running this small hardware store for years now. A couple of easygoing, middle-aged guys, they tended to mind their own business, so to speak, but were nonetheless attentive to their customers.

"Hello, Tom. It's that time of the year again, huh?"

"Yep, summer has arrived. I sure love this country. How have you boys been?"

"Not too bad," they both answered in unison.

Uncle Tom placed the summer's propane order, while trying to exact a guarantee that it would be delivered the same day.

"You understand that I have to contend with the general?" he said, referring to Auntie.

"We understand, Tom, but, unfortunately, we can't guarantee that it'll be there tonight, but definitely tomorrow morning."

Shrugging his shoulder, Uncle Tom looked at me and said, "Well, I guess that's the best that we can do, Toulaki." Taking me by the hand, Uncle Tom started for the door.

"See you later, boys—and thanks. I'll see you tomorrow for sure, right, if not sooner?"

"You betcha, Tom. Glad to see you back. Bye, bye little girl."

Jack and Ron both waved goodbye to me. I smiled and gave them a little wave in return. Then, we went to the grocery store next door and ordered blocks of ice for the ice box.

"So, what happened? Are they coming?" Auntie asked as we walked through the front door.

"They couldn't promise it'd be here tonight, but definitely by tomorrow."

"Oh, what are we going to do? The meat will spoil."

"I don't think it will, but even if it does, we'll just throw it out and buy a fresh pound of hamburger meat."

"I hate wasting food." Auntie lamented.

"There's nothing more that we can do. If not tonight, they'll definitely deliver in the morning. We'll go out to dinner tonight. I saw a little café, as I was driving in. I think it's new—at least it's the first time I've seen it."

"But, we can't go out tonight; what if they come?"

"We'll leave the back door open for the iceman. The propone is no problem; they'll hook it up outside. They have done this before; they know what to do. We can even leave them a note if that'll make you feel better."

Auntie calmed down, for she could see the logic in what Uncle Tom was saying.

"I just need a little time to relax before we go out to dinner," Uncle Tom said.

"Toula, here are the car keys. There's a grocery bag in the backseat. Could you bring it in, please?"

"Sure, Uncle Tom."

The grocery bag contained a six pack of Miller, apples, a watermelon, corn on the cob and a package of tootsie rolls. Uncle Tom's beloved t-bone steaks were wrapped in butcher paper. I put the bag on the kitchen counter, took out a bottle of beer, opened it and then brought it to my uncle. Although I knew it might ruin my appetite, I unwrapped a tootsie roll, and popped it into my mouth. Uncle Tom settled into one of the leather chairs in the living room, took a gulp of beer, and then looked for the newspaper.

"Tootsie, could you look in the bag again and see if I brought the newspaper in?" I didn't remember seeing the newspaper, but I checked anyway.

"No, Uncle Tom, there's no paper in the bag."

"Hmm, I must have left it in the car. Could you check for me, please? Here are the keys again." Before I even opened the car door, I could see the newspaper in the back seat. I grabbed it, and locked the car door. I handed the paper and keys to Uncle Tom.

"Thanks, tootsie."

After reading the paper for no more than ten minutes, Uncle Tom fell asleep, snoring loudly.

"Let him sleep a while. He's had a long day." Auntie sounded sympathetic.

"We'll get ready in the meantime."

Uncle Tom woke up about fifteen minutes later, awakened by his own snoring, no doubt.

"What happened?" asked Uncle Tom, blinking, and looking a little confused.

"You fell asleep, that's what happened," Auntie said. "Do you feel better now?

You sure you want to go out for dinner?"

"Yes, yes, let's go."

"Now, where are my car keys?" he asked, still looking a little dazed.

"Right there, next to you, on the side table," Auntie said.

"Oh, yeah. Okay, let's go before it gets too dark. I'm starving; I haven't eaten since noon."

He looked at his watch; it was just about seven o'clock.

"Oh my—seven hours without food. No wonder I feel so weak."

We got into Uncle Tom's car and drove to Ruby's Café. It was a cozy, friendly little place, with no more than a dozen tables, each one sporting a red and white plastic checkered table cloth, and a small glass vase each holding a fresh red rose. The place was almost empty; there was just a young couple sitting at a table by the window. Before we had time to get comfortable, the waitress arrived with three menus.

"Hello, folks. New in town? Welcome. Can I get you all something to drink, while you look at the menu?"

Uncle Tom looked at Auntie and then at me.

"I'll have a bottle of Miller."

"A glass of red wine for me, please," Auntie said.

"And, I'll have a coke." I said.

"Thanks folks, I'll be right back with your refreshments," the waitress said

Scanning the menu of standard American fare, I chose fried chicken and mashed potatoes. Uncle Tom had a t-bone steak, 'natch, and a baked potato, and Auntie ordered meatloaf and mashed potatoes. Steamed vegetables came with all of the orders. We made small talk until the food arrived.

"So, how was your drive, Tom?"

"Not bad. There was a little traffic. Can't complain," he responded, reaching for his bottle of beer.

"I wish Toula would stay awake and keep me company. She slept most of the way."

"I can't help it; the car rocks me to sleep." "I know, I know," Uncle Tom chuckled.

The waitress brought our food to the table; we dug right in.

"Good food, don't you think?" Uncle Tom said, directing his comments to no one in particular.

"Yes, yes, it's a nice little restaurant, Tom. Good service, reasonable prices," Auntie responded.

They both seemed satisfied.

"We should come back," he continued.

"Yes, we should," she agreed.

It was dark when we left Ruby's. Looking up at the star-filled sky, I could feel sleep coming on. We drove home, tired but content. Once back at The Cottage, we went straight to bed. It had been a long, busy day.

The ice and propane men had both come and gone before we got up the following morning. Auntie was thrilled as she placed the food in the frosty ice box. Uncle Tom turned the thermostat on, taking the chill out of the house. Auntie switched on the large gas stove to prepare pancakes, bacon and eggs. Coffee was brewing as I walked into the kitchen. The house had come alive and felt so—well, homey. We had a leisurely breakfast and looked forward to the rest of the weekend.

Port Huron was a small, friendly town. Several hundred people lived there year-round, but twice as many came on weekends during the summer months. The town was just a stone's throw from the beach where people swam, water skied, sunbathed, and just plain relaxed. The town boasted a couple of small grocery stores, a gift shop, a hardware store, an art gallery, and couple of small restaurants. People dressed casually, of course, wearing bathing suits, shorts, t-shirts, and sun dresses; some wore hats to shield their faces from the hot sun.

We usually walked into town to do our shopping. I always made sure to get an Eskimo pie, a treat I had grown up eating in the village. In summer, the good humor man would come to Skopi every Saturday afternoon. I would run as fast as I could to the town square, money in hand, when I heard him blow his whistle. Gosh, how I loved biting into the cold vanilla ice cream! The crisp chocolate outer layer would break into little chocolate shards around my mouth. Making sure not to lose a crumb, I'd use my tongue to gather up every last little bit.

We would walk to the lake a couple of blocks away. Along the water front there was a medium-size beach. The fairly rough sand and small stones made it a little difficult to walk. The lake itself was clear, clean and cool. We would wade into the shallow water picking up small, uniquely-shaped pebbles and shells from the sandy bottom. Once we got used to the cold water, we would enjoy leisurely swims. The beach was never crowded, at least not where we would typically set up.

We'd bring food, drinks, games, and reading material. And, of course, our beach umbrella. We'd spent a good portion of the day there.

Sometimes Auntie and I would play canasta or gin rummy. When there were enough of us, we would play monopoly as well. Auntie would also knit, read and write letters. Uncle Tom and I would pass the time reading our favorite magazines. He enjoyed reading US News and World Report while I occupied myself with fashion magazines and comic books. Uncle Tom would always end up dozing the afternoon away.

There was a roller skating rink across the street from The Cottage; that's where I learned to roller skate. I would go there practically every Friday and Saturday night. I enjoyed roller-skating and meeting friends there. The boys were always eager to teach me how to skate.

"*Here let me help*," they'd say, placing one arm around my waist and the other on my arm, guiding me along. I had never been in such close physical contact with boys before. It made me feel both nervous, and excited. I knew Mother definitely would not have approved. But, instead of imagining my mother's dirty looks, I concentrated on staying upright. As much as I enjoyed roller skating, I enjoyed the attention from the boys even more.

We frequently invited my girlfriends Darlene, Betty and Sharon to The Cottage. Auntie would occasionally invite her friends too. Uncle Tom's nephews from Boston and Chicago would also spend time with us at this magical place. Peopled came to The Cottage and forgot their troubles for a while.

Weather permitting—and, if he was in the mood—Uncle Tom would grill hamburgers and hot dogs on the barbecue. Auntie and I would make potato salad. Irene and Helen, our closest neighbors, and their spouses, lived just a few yards away. Like Auntie and Uncle Tom, they were in their sixties and retired. They lived at the great lake year-round. They would come over and visit most weekends. Auntie and Uncle Tom would often invite them to stay for dinner, especially when Uncle Tom barbequed. They would usually bring a side dish, or a bouquet of flowers, or something from their garden. Sometimes they would stick around after dinner and play bridge with Uncle Tom and Auntie. I enjoyed their visits. They paid a lot of attention to me, which could even get a little embarrassing at times.

"My, how you have grown, young lady," one or the other would say. *"You have such lovely hair, nice and thick and curly. Whom did you get your hair from? How is school? You must be so happy to be on summer vacation, huh? Pretty soon all the boys will be after you, you are s-o-o-o pretty."*

I have very special memories of The Cottage and often wonder how it has weathered the years. The setting was positively magical! I hope one day to visit this wonderful place again.

Wilkins Elementary

Summer was coming to an end. The first day of school was just a couple of weeks away.

"You need more school clothes, Toula. Let's concentrate on getting you some warm winter clothes," Auntie said. "You are going to need an overcoat, a wool cap, boots, mittens, earmuffs, several sweaters and skirts, and knee length socks. Unlike the mild winters of Greece, it gets very cold here. I don't know if you know that?"

The clothes we ended up buying at Hudson's this time were even uglier than those we had bought three months earlier shortly after I had arrived from Greece. I literally cringed as Auntie chose each piece of clothing. She overruled all my objections, however, making it clear she knew what she was doing—not that she did. *At least, I'll be warm,* I thought sarcastically. I shuddered at the thought of facing my peers in those clothes.

"You are going to need a nice school bag, Toula, don't you think?"

We took the escalator down to the basement for the school supplies. She quickly eyed an ugly brown and white checkered bag. She threw in the bag half-dozen no. 2 pencils, a bunch of black and white pens, a notebook, and a package of crayons. And, there was still more! She bought me a colorful new metal lunch box with a small thermos, no less. You can imagine how ugly the whole get-up was. How was I going to face my new classmates? I tried not thinking of my old friends in Skopi, knowing that if they could see me, they would never stop laughing. I absolutely dreaded the first day of class.

But, that day—the first Tuesday after Labor Day—arrived on schedule anyway. I got up around six-thirty in the morning with the usual great big knot in my belly. I got busy getting ready for a day that would surely be quite difficult.

Since I had taken a bath the night before, I splashed some water on my face, brushed my teeth, and combed my hair. I slipped on the clothes Auntie had laid out for me the night before. I hurried downstairs for breakfast. A bowl of steaming oatmeal, a cup of hot cocoa and a glass of milk were waiting for me on the kitchen table. I didn't have much of an appetite, however, thanks to my anxiety.

Auntie helped me put on my three quarter length overcoat with the fake fur collar. She buttoned every button—all four of them—for me. I could barely move. It felt like I was wearing a straight jacket. I grabbed my school bag along with my lunch box. Darlene was waiting for us on the porch when we opened the front door. She was going to ride with us to school.

"Hi Darlene," I called out nervously.

Seeing my friend calmed me a bit.

"Hi, Toula, all ready for school?"

"I'm not sure to be honest. How 'bout you?"

"I'm okay, I guess. Hey, what's with the get-up?"

"I know, I know."

We walked to Auntie's car parked out front. We got in the backseat, throwing our school bags on the floor in front of us.

"So, how are you today, Darlene?" asked Auntie. "My, you look awfully pretty. Are you ready for school?" Auntie adjusted the rear view mirror so that she could see us in the back.

"Thank you. I guess I'm about as ready as I'll ever be. My mom didn't have time to buy all the things that I'll need, but I guess I'll be okay."

"Good, good. Now, remember to be good girls and study hard."
Darlene and I looked at one another, rolled our eyes, and giggled.

"Yes, Mrs. Siakotos."

I continued feeling pretty nervous, not knowing, really, what to expect.
I concluded that my first day was not going to go well. I was so worried
that I could barely think straight. I worried about how I looked, how I
sounded—what with my heavy Greek accent. I also wondered whether I
would fit in. Would the other kids be nice to me? Would my teacher be
young and kind, or old and mean? Would I be able to do the required
school work?

Not only was I sick to my stomach, I had a splitting headache too, by
the time Auntie pulled up across the street from school. I was afraid that
I might throw up.

The three of us crossed the street together. Once inside, Darlene
rushed off to her homeroom. Taking me by the hand, Auntie marched
toward the receptionist.

"Excuse me, this is my niece Toula, Toula Siakotos. Could you please
check and see where she should go?"

The receptionist looked at me and then checked the school roster on
her desk. She came out from behind her desk and took me by the hand.

"It's alright, Mrs. Siakotos. I'll take Toula to her homeroom upstairs.
Today is a half day; school will let out at noon."

Auntie bent down and kissed me on the cheek and said, "I'll be here
at noon to pick you up. This nice lady will show you to your classroom."

My face—nay, my entire person felt flush from embarrassment.
I hoped that no one had noticed. If I could have disappeared into the
woodwork, I would have gladly done so.

The receptionist led me upstairs. My homeroom was the first one on
the right. The door was open. The teacher, Mrs. McKenzie, a middle-
aged woman with a short, brown perm smiled as the receptionist ushered

me in. *But, this can't be right,* I thought at once, as it was quite obvious the children in the room were half my age. They looked to be about six years old. They were not sitting at regular desks but in small chairs placed around short, round tables. I looked at the blackboard that covered one wall; the alphabet was written in capital and lowercase letters at the very top as were the cardinal numbers, from one to ten. *This is first grade,* I thought. *What am I doing here?* I had completed the sixth grade in my country, so I should have been in the seventh grade, not in first!

I felt upset and humiliated. I was convinced that a mistake had been made. I checked with the teacher and she in turn checked the roster. Unfortunately, there had been no mistake. I was in the right room. I had been assigned to her class. The kids looked at me in confusion. I wanted to run away. I felt extremely uncomfortable. *I was in the wrong class,* I kept telling myself.

"Class, class," the teacher called out after a few minutes. "Please, find your seats, and please remain silent." I reluctantly made myself sit with the other kids around the small round table. I looked straight ahead, too afraid to look at the other kids, certain that every eye was focused on me. The teacher began class by calling out our names. Coming to my name, she made the following announcement:

"Your classmate Toula is new to America. She is from a country in Europe called Greece. She completed the sixth grade in her country, but she is here with us because she needs to learn the English language. Let's make her feel welcome."

I doubt they understood considering their age, but I was relieved that at least an explanation had been given as to why I was in the room with them. We spent the morning printing part of the alphabet, and coloring figures and objects on paper. Then, half-way through the morning we had milk and cookies. *Oh, My God, this is so humiliating,* I thought, sitting around with the lilliputians.

Right then and there I decided the only way out of this nightmare was to learn English as quickly as I possibly could. I couldn't wait for the first day of school to end. But, there was still one more humiliation to endure before I could go home and bury my head under the bed covers. Although I didn't look all that different from the other kids—we were all dressed pretty nerdy—I sure did sound a whole lot different. When I spoke with my thick foreign accent, everyone looked at me as though I was from another planet, which, of course, I was in a way. Given that I wanted to be like everyone else, I decided I would not speak another word unless it was absolutely necessary. And on those occasions when speaking was unavoidable, I would do so as briefly as possible.

And so, I was forced to give up my fantasies of returning to Greece. I needed to learn English—and the sooner the better. I figured that once I got a handle on the language, I could catch up with my peers. This became my one and only goal. To this end, I sought the help of my aunt and uncle and my friend Darlene. I listened to the radio and watched TV, and tried to read English as much as I could.

With my English rapidly improving, I began skipping grades—going from first to third, and then to the fourth grade. I even won the spelling bee while in fourth grade; I'm not sure how I did it, but my name was on the blackboard for one week as both proof and reward. I then moved on to the sixth grade, and, before the school year was over, I was in the seventh grade, where I belonged. It felt as though I was running a marathon and I could not stop until I reached the finishing line.

It was a stressful and challenging year. I was forced to confront the new reality of my life. I was in America to stay whether I liked it or not. It was time to get off the fence and start adjusting to a new country; I began to feel more in control as a result. I began—albeit ambivalently—to engage with my new life. I held out hope, however, that one day I would return to Greece, my homeland, but now was not the time.

I made a couple of new friends in school. Along with Darlene, Sharon and Betty would remain my closest friends throughout elementary and secondary schools. We joined the same high school sorority, Phi Beta Chi. We had slumber parties and stayed at one another's houses, went to the movies, shopping, to the beach, and talked on the 'phone. We attended various school dances together and triple-dated with our boyfriends. We experimented with makeup and various different hairstyles. We talked about our menstrual periods and how to manage our monthly cramps. We bitched and complained about our families. On my own, I tried smoking by pilfering Chesterfields from the pack Auntie kept in her bedroom. She soon caught wind of that, as it were, and put a stop to it.

These dear friends, and my high school sweetheart Wayne, helped me navigate a very difficult time in my life, at a very challenging developmental age, adolescence. My friends and I stayed in touch for many years after we graduated from high school. Although our lives took different directions, I think of them from to time with warmth and gratitude.

The Letter

It had been four months since I left Greece—and still no word from my family. I felt sad, lonely and not a little annoyed with them. I struggled not to feel abandoned, forgotten. At the same time, I feared that something had happened to them.

Finally, one day in late September upon returning home from school, I found a letter in the mail box. The letter was addressed to Uncle Tom; it was from my cousin Chris. The eldest son of Panagiota, my father's eldest sister, Chris had come to America several years earlier. He had settled in Chicago where he married his childhood sweetheart, Zoe. A tall, handsome man in his early thirties, he worked as a waiter at a Greek restaurant in downtown Chicago. Having left his parents and many siblings behind in order to make a go of it in America, he was expected to help support them by regularly sending money to Greece. It was also expected that he would sponsor as many relatives as he could.

I hoped that the letter included news of my family. Waiting for Uncle Tom to come home from work, I became increasingly anxious about the contents of the letter. When I heard the side door open, I rushed toward my uncle, letter in hand.

"Uncle Tom, Uncle Tom, a letter from Chicago came for you today. It's from cousin Chris. Shall I open it and read it to you?"

"Give me just a moment to change, and I'll be right up."

As was his habit upon returning home from work, he went to the basement to change into comfortable clothes. He then slowly climbed back up the stairs and walked into the kitchen, where he opened the refrigerator door. Withdrawing a bottle of Miller, he then went into the living room and stretched out on the red recliner. I followed him like a little dog waiting for a milk bone. I could barely contain my excitement.

"Alright now, you can read the letter to me." I tore open the envelope, withdrew the letter and began reading:

> *Dear Uncle Tom, Aunt Anna and cousin Toula,* Chris wrote in Greek.
>
> *I hope my letter finds you well, as we too are well . . .*

After some brief remarks of their *happy lives* in Chicago, he wrote the following:

> *I am sorry to report that Aunt Georgia, Toula's mother, was arrested for murder a couple of months ago. The police say she killed the old man who murdered Uncle Adonis . . .*

In disbelief, I read that part of the sentence again . . . *arrested for murder.* I let the letter fall from my hands. I felt my body go limp. Uncle Tom calmly wrapped his big, strong arms around me, gently patting me on the head.

"There, there, now, everything will be okay—you'll see. There must be some mistake. Your mamma could not have done such a thing." Auntie rushed into the living room from the kitchen.

"What's going on? Why is everyone so quiet?"

Uncle Tom looked at her, shook his head in sadness, and handed her the letter which he had picked up from the floor.

Realizing what I had just read, I started to cry, slowly at first and then hysterically.

"No, no, it can't be!" I screamed. "Not my manoula!"

Auntie took me in her arms. I felt like running out of the house into the street and never stopping.

When will this tragedy end? I asked myself. *My family must be cursed.*

How terrible for my mother. Hasn't she suffered enough already? What is going to happen to her? How long is she going to be in jail? How is she being treated? Who is taking care of the house and the land? The questions kept on coming, but there were no answers.

Uncle Tom and Auntie looked at me helplessly. They didn't have any answers for me either. Retrieving the letter from the table, and through a veil of tears I began reading anew:

> *It happened soon after little Toula had left the village. The old man was found dead by the police in the courtyard of Theia's house. His body and clothing were bloody. Theia Georgia also had blood on her clothes, face and arms. A neighbor, Saldarena, and her young daughter Yanoula from across the way saw the whole thing and called the police. They arrived at the scene and placed them under arrest—Theia Georgia, Uncle George and Gus—locking them up in jail in Tripoli. After several days Uncle George and Gus were released, but things don't look good for Theia Georgia. She has been in jail ever since, awaiting trial. I have no other information, but I will let you know as soon as I hear more.*

I let the letter fall to the floor again and ran to my room. Slamming the door shut, I fell on my knees. Making sure I was facing east, the proper orientation for prayer, I clasped my hands tightly. I closed my eyes and started reciting the Lord's prayer. I pleaded with God, the Virgin Mary,

Christ, and Saint Nickolas to watch over my mother. I then took out a pen and paper and began composing a letter.

> *Dear Gus,*
>
> *I just learned from our cousin Chris that Mother has been arrested for murder! I know this cannot be possible! It's a terrible mistake! It has to be! How is she holding up? Is she in good health? I worry about her so much. Do you visit her daily? Do you bring her favorite food, feta, kefaloteri—her special cheeses—lakerda, the smoked fish that she likes so much—loukoumi—her favorite sweet; food that she enjoys but never has enough money to buy. Please, make sure that you and Yianni visit her every day, and please hug and kiss her for me. And by the way, does she have an attorney? And, when will the trial take place?*

Suddenly, I felt like a grown up, so anxious for my mother that I was giving orders to my older brothers.

> *Please, write and let me know exactly what happened as soon as you receive my letter. I'll be anxiously awaiting your response.*
>
> *I'm praying for Mother every day. I know God is watching over her.*

> *Your loving sister,*
> *Toula*

I slowly walked from my bedroom downstairs in a kind of trance, wondering how such a terrible thing could have happened. Everything seemed fine here in Detroit, same as always: Uncle Tom in his chair reading the paper and puffing on his pipe. Auntie in the kitchen getting dinner ready. I felt out of place by contrast, worried, and alone. I could not dispel these feelings as much as I tried. Auntie looked up at me tenderly. It comforted me a bit how sad and concerned she was.

"Tom, dinner is ready," she called out. "Toula, you must be hungry; you haven't eaten since lunch. Come, sit down and have your dinner."

We all took our seats around the table. Uncle Tom took a gulp of beer. Auntie dug into her favorite spaghetti, but without her usual enthusiasm. I moved the food on my plate around with my fork. I tried getting something down, but I was just too upset and preoccupied. After a couple of minutes, I put my fork down and didn't pick it up again. Worried, they both encouraged me to eat, but they soon realized that it was of no use.

"I have written a letter to Gus. I'd like to drop it in the mail box down the block."

"I can mail the letter for you in the morning on the way to work," Uncle Tom offered.

"That's okay, thank you. I'd prefer mailing it right a way. I need to know what really happened as soon as possible."

They understood, so I grabbed the letter and rushed out the door. I felt a little better being outside in the fresh air alone with my thoughts. I was walking quite fast and soon started running. A few children were still playing out on the sidewalk. Looking up at the star-filled night, I quietly began—again—to recite the Lord's prayer, pleading with the Almighty: *Please Lord, watch over my manoula.* Picking up speed, I quickly reached the blue mailbox. I checked to see when my letter would be picked up; unfortunately, I had missed the last pick-up of the day.

I guess it'll have to wait till tomorrow, I thought, feeling disappointed. I continued running for several more blocks. I tried to clear my mind, but it felt dense, a mass of confusion. I couldn't think clearly. Tears began streaming down my cheeks. I knew I had to get back home, but I just wanted to keep running. I slowed down as the house came into view. I entered from the side door and quickly said goodnight, rushing upstairs to my room.

I changed into my nightgown, washed my face, brushed my teeth and got into bed. Just as I was about to drift off into sleep, I saw an apparition of the old man who had killed my father standing at the threshold of my bedroom. The ghost had long, wispy white hair and a beard just like the old man. He was draped in a long, white robe, his face eerie white. I looked at it, wondering if I wasn't dreaming. Within seconds, I felt the pressure of two hands, one on each side of my face, holding the bed sheet tightly across my face. I couldn't breathe; I was suffocating. Flailing my arms, and gasping for air, I pulled the sheet off my face. I reached for the lamp on the nightstand with a trembling hand and switched on the light. Terrified, I looked around, and in a loud voice ordered whoever—or whatever—was in my room to leave immediately.

I tried to calm my agitated mind by means of an inner dialogue:

It is okay. You are just imagining things. You are under a lot of stress. It is all right. You are safe. You can relax now.

I kept repeating this little mantra till my breath slowed and my body stopped shaking. I crossed myself a number of times, imploring God, the Virgin Mary, Saint Nickolas and my father to watch over me.

News from Home

It had been two weeks since I had written but I still had not heard from my brother Gus. I continued to worry about and pray for my mother. I just couldn't understand how she could be considered a suspect in Kalimanis' death. There was no doubt in my mind that my mother had absolutely nothing to do with it.

Mother had suffered a great deal in life. In my view, she had dealt with each setback in a relatively constructive way. My mother was not a violent person. I had never seen her act out her anger. I could not even recall my mother ever striking us children no matter how unnerving our behavior. She dealt with difficult situations by turning inward, becoming quiet and introspective. At times we would catch her sobbing. Talking with her husband and to her sons Nick and Gus helped her cope with rough patches.

Staying in control was important to Mother. She held to her principles. She didn't relinquish her responsibilities. She was a proud, independent woman. She had integrity and exercised good judgment. She believed in herself and in her family, that together we could survive anything no matter what.

She would become mistrustful, almost paranoid, when insecure, however. Her fundamental mistrust of people became more pronounced in hard times. For example, she would address us in a whisper. She made sure the doors and windows to the house were kept shut. She became alarmed when there was a knock on the door, making sure she knew who it was before answering. She ventured out of the house only when necessary, speaking very little—if at all—with the so called outsiders, i.e. friends, neighbors and locals. She instructed us to do the same—that is, not to speak to anyone when out of the house and to return home as soon as possible. I can't say if my siblings did as my mother instructed, but I sure did. I didn't question her, believing there was something to fear out there in the big, bad world. I trusted my mother. I felt safe having her in charge.

Despite the cynicism, Mother could be loving, empathic and compassionate. She would never turn her back on anyone in need; she would share what she had, no matter how little. Here too, however, she would be on guard, fearful of being taken advantage. She would determine how much she could afford to contribute and would stick with that decision, even though she might have been asked to give more.

Finally, a letter from home appeared in the mailbox.

Dearest sister Toula,

First of all, please accept my apologies for not writing sooner. How long has it been since you left home—four or five months? How are you? How are you being treated? Have you started school, and, if so, how is your English coming along?

You know, Mother talks about you almost every day. She still feels that you were too young to leave the family; she tends to blame herself for that. But, not to worry, we are all fine, even Mother.

About a week after you left, yet another fight broke out among the foniades—murderers. As you well know, this has always been very upsetting, so we started our chores early. Yianni left early for work. I was on the terrace having breakfast before school, and Mother was in the courtyard sweeping. We heard screams and fisticuffs coming from the house behind ours, then the slamming of their front door. There was an eerie silence for several minutes when suddenly we heard a banging on our front door. I got up from my chair and looked toward the front door. I could see the old man, Kalimanis at the courtyard door. Mother stopped sweeping. We looked at one another anxiously. I knew we needed to help him, so I asked Mother to open the door.

She resisted. I could see the anger, the confusion in her eyes. 'What are you asking me to do—help the man who killed your father? No, I will not do it!' I urged her to open the door. She crossed her arms defiantly and shook her head no.

'Then, I will come down and open it myself,' I threatened. At that point—I assume to protect me—she reluctantly opened the door. I was horrified by what I saw. The old man, covered in blood, had been leaning on the door, barely holding himself up. Once Mother opened the door, he fell right on top of her, knocking her to the ground. This was truly shocking. I rushed downstairs. His head and clothes were a bloody mess. Mother's entire person was covered in his blood. With the old man's head resting on her lap, Mother sat motionless on the ground in shock. I pulled her away as one would pull at a mannequin.

The old man was now lying on the ground, blood coming out of the right side of his mouth. I realized he was dead the moment I placed my hand on his forehead. It was a frightening sight; his eyes were still wide open, his long, white hair matted with blood, his face and arms bruised.

I was trying to comfort Mother. I picked up a rag that I found on the ground, and began cleaning Kalimani's blood off her person. The police arrived at about the same time. I was surprised to see them arrive so quickly—who had called them? Incredibly, they accused mother of killing the old man. As for the motive? To avenge our father's murder. I was outraged by their accusations and tried to explain what

had really happened, but they would have none of it. They said they
had been told by the neighbors what had actually happened.

'They saw your mother kill the old man,' the police said.'

While demanding that the police let Mother go, I happened
to look out of the open front door. That crazy Saldarena and her
daughter Yanoula were looking directly into our courtyard. Of course,
the usual suspects, I thought. Saldarena and her family were known
in the village as troublemakers. A crowd started to gather, gawking,
mumbling and crossing themselves.

The police handcuffed Mother and me, placed us in the police
car and took us to jail in Tripoli. Later they arrested Uncle George,
too. They said he was the 'brains' behind the murder. He and I were
interrogated over the course of three days before being released. Mother,
however, is still in jail awaiting trial.

She's doing surprisingly well considering. You know how Mother
is; she copes well. She is well liked by both the guards and her fellow
prisoners. She has taken a special interest in a pregnant young woman
who attacked her abusive husband in self-defense.

People from all over are in an uproar over this injustice. They
come and visit Mother, bringing her food, flowers, pastries, icons, gold
and silver crucifixes. Father Manolis visits Mother on a weekly basis,
blessing her and praying for her early release.

Mother, true to her nature, shares whatever she is given with
everyone in jail, including the guards. She even got the priest to give
weekly liturgy services at the prison right after regular Sunday service.

It is amazing Toulaki how things are evolving. People are
protesting Mother's incarceration. They feel she has been victimized yet
again. They demand she be released immediately. One of the prisoners
has even written a song about Mother's plight; he calls it "Georgia" in
her honor. Of course, she looks forward to the day she's released and

allowed to return home. She worries about us and about the house and the land. Uncle George has hired an attorney, but, unfortunately, a trial won't begin till March or April of next year; that's a very long time to wait, but there doesn't seem to be anything that we can do to expedite the matter.

Don't worry, we visit her everyday as do many others, and, yes, we bring her favorite food. She sends her love. Enclosed you'll find a brief note from her.

Your loving brother,
Gus

My dear little daughter Toula,

I hope my letter finds you happy and well. I miss you very much. I know we will be together again very soon. Your brother has explained what's happened, so I won't bore you with the awful details. Please, don't worry about me. I'm doing fine—really! Take good care of yourself and say hello to your uncle and aunt for me. Please kiss and thank them for me for taking such good care of you.

Hugs and Kisses,
Manoula

I held both letters to my chest and sobbed uncontrollably. I read them over and over until I had every word memorized. The longing to be with my family was indescribable!

I wrote back immediately, thanking them for their letters and expressing relief that Mother had nothing to do with the old man's death—not that there was ever a doubt, mind you. Still, it worried me that she was in jail and would be there for sometime to come.

The Trial

Mother's incarceration grabbed headlines not just in Skopi but throughout the Peloponnesus. Thanks to radio, newspapers—and plain old word of mouth—Mother's plight remained fresh in people's minds and hearts. The jailhouse-penned tune "Georgia" was recorded and played on the radio. Mother became something of a local legend.

The following is Gus' account of the trial:

Finally, the day of the trial had arrived. The trial took place in the courthouse in Tripoli on Thursday, April 24, 1953; it lasted four days.

The judge, Mr. Manolaos—middle-aged, short, balding, fastidious—was known to be tough but fair. He was from Sparta, about thirty-five miles southeast of Tripoli. He was married, but not much else was known about him. It looked as though he carried an entire career's worth of documents inside the worn leather briefcase he carried with him into court.

The district attorney, Mr. Katsikis, was a tall, wiry, bespectacled young man. He was around thirty years of age. He was born in Kalamata, about ninety miles southwest of Tripoli. He had graduated from the University of Athens. At that time, he had just a couple of years of trial experience. He lived in Tripoli with his wife and young daughter.

Mr. Mihalis, a criminal defense lawyer with over ten years of experience, was Mother's attorney. He was about forty, tall and good-looking. He dressed immaculately and wore his thick black hair slicked back. Like Mr.

Katsikis, he lived in Tripoli with his wife, young son and daughter.

The courtroom was vibrating with people. The large crowd spilled out into the street. People pushed and pulled at one another, craning their necks to see inside the courtroom. Some looky-loos actually brought chairs and stools from home so they could have a better view of the proceedings. The police continually tooted their whistles, trying to keep the outside mob in order.

Inside the courtroom, two bailiffs repeatedly asked people to remain seated and to lower their voices. Even after all the seats were taken, people still tried to force their way inside the courtroom. The bailiff had to shove them back outside.

The trial, as expected, started late. Spectators started to grow impatient, shouting for the trial to begin. *Ela tora, ela tora,* they shouted.

Mother was already in the courtroom, sitting next to her attorney. As she had requested, Uncle George was allowed to sit next to her. She wore her customary black dress and shoes. Her hair, as usual, was parted down the middle, braided and pinned in a bun. She had placed a black *mantili* loosely over her hair securing it with a small knot just under her chin. She looked pale and had lost a few pounds, looking thinner than usual. Her expression was somber. She held a small, white, embroidered handkerchief. Effie, Gus and John sat directly behind her along with a group of extended relatives. There were many familiar and friendly faces in the courtroom.

Finally, the courtroom came to order. Mr. Katsikis called his first witness, a woman in the village who had known Mother all of her life. A fifty-four year old married mother of four, Mrs. Kokkinis had just become a grandmother. Often struggling to make ends meet, she and her husband had occasionally asked my parents for help.

After Mrs. Kokkinis was sworn in, Mr. Katsikis began his examination.

"Now, Mrs. Kokkinis, how long have you known the defendant?"

"All of my life. She and I were born and raised in this town. I have known her over fifty years."

"Tell me then, what kind of a person is the defendant?"

"To tell you the truth, I don't know who she really is. She is arrogant and aloof. She hardly acknowledges me when our paths cross."

"Do you think the defendant is capable of killing anyone? Do you think she killed the deceased?"

"Anything is possible."

People in the gallery reacted audibly to her testimony, some in apparent agreement with the witness' testimony. Mother twisted her handkerchief slightly. My siblings reached for one another's hands.

Judge Manolaos pounded his gavel, demanding quiet in the courtroom. After a few more preliminary questions, the witness was cross-examined.

Mr. Mihalis stood up, buttoning his doubled breasted pin-striped black suit, and began to cross-examine Mrs. Kokkinis.

"You say you hardly know the defendant?"

"Yes, that's what I said."

"I understand that you and your husband visited the defendant and her late husband, a number of times. Mrs. Siakotos would welcome you and your husband into her home and serve food and plenty of wine. Isn't that true Mrs. Kokkinis?"

"Well, there were a few times when we knocked on her door. We hoped that we might have a little taste of the late Adonis' good wine. He was a pretty good winemaker, you know," she testified, her eyes gleaming. "May God rest his soul," she continued, crossing herself.

People in the courtroom roared with laughter. It was a well known fact in Skopi that the Kokkinis' liked to partake of the grape.

"Quiet, quiet," the judge thundered, pounding his gavel.

"And, isn't it a fact that the defendant allowed your family to plant on her land—free of rent—on more than one occasion?"

"Well, yes, I guess that's true."

"And, isn't it also a fact that Gus, the defendant's youngest son, tutored your son with his school work on a number of occasions, so that he might be promoted to the next grade? Isn't that true, Mrs. Kokkinis?"

With her head lowered, she mumbled, "Yes, it is true."

Witness after witness, the testimony against Mother was discredited.

Finally, the witnesses who alleged that they saw Mother kill the old man Kalimanis took the stand. First, Saldarena and then her daughter, Yanoula stated that they did indeed see Mother kill him.

During cross-examination, however, they were unable to say how Mother killed him. *Did she shoot him? Did she stab him with a knife? Did she strangle him with her bare hands? What weapon exactly did the defendant use to kill the deceased?* They couldn't answer any of these important questions for they didn't see a weapon. As a matter of fact, their house was at such a distance—over fifty yards from the crime scene—that they had to admit that they were not exactly sure what they saw other than Kalimanis pounding on the door, the door opening and him and Mother falling to the ground. Furthermore, the daughter's version was somewhat different from her mother's.

The trial went so well that Mother didn't even have to testify. Mother, of course, was acquitted, and was immediately released from custody. We all breathed a huge sigh of relief. We hugged and kissed one another. We thanked God, and Mr. Mihalis. Mother made the sign of the cross three times, and recited Bible passages under her breath. She thanked Mr. Mihalis over and over before reaching out and kissing him on both cheeks. She then took from her pocket several pieces of colorfully wrapped hard candy and handed them to him, saying, "These are for your beautiful children. May they live a long life." He thanked her, gave her a big hug, and wished her *kali tixi*, good luck.

Mother was mobbed when she walked out of the courthouse. People gathered around, handing her bouquets of flowers, candy and small orthodox icons. They wished her and her family well.

Mother, Uncle George, Effie, Nick, Yianni, and Gus all piled into a taxi for the trip back to Skopi. Aware of the story, the driver congratulated Mother, shook everyone's hand, and announced that the fare was on him.

We responded with a loud *euxaristo,* thank you.

As we approached Skopi, we could see the locals waiting at the foot of the village, for Mother's return. As the cab slowed, they reached in to shake Mother's hand and to give her still more gifts of flowers, homemade bread and sweets.

"*Kalosorises,*" welcome home, we have missed you.

Mother, her eyes welling up with tears, responded by saying, "Thank you, and thanks to the good Lord for making my return to my home and family possible. May God bless all of you." With tears rolling down her cheeks, she crossed herself several more times as the taxi came to a stop in front of our home . . ."

Mother's Depression

Mother had been in jail for nearly seven months. Although she was treated well and received a great deal of support from the community, being incarcerated nonetheless had taken a tremendous toll on her.

Gus wrote in great detail, and, rather uncharacteristically, with much feeling about the depression that descended upon Mother after her release:

> *I have never seen Mother so depressed. Of course, she has been depressed before, but never like this. It's different this time, worse, deeper. She has become quiet, withdrawn. She has taken to her bed. She has difficulty sleeping at night, and takes short naps throughout the day. She is restless and can't seem to relax. At times she even cries out in her sleep.*
>
> *Her appetite is almost non-existent. She has become quite thin. In the morning she'll drink a cup of tea with a little honey and eat a small piece of bread dipped in the tea. She eats very little at midday and at dinner time. We have bought her favorite foods: rice, feta and kefalotiri cheeses, sardines, dried cod, and lamb. We bring her homegrown produce; tomatoes, cucumbers, lettuce, parsley, green garlic, and small green onions for salad. Knowing how much she enjoys herbal fragrances, fresh mint, oregano and sweet basil are always in the house. Yianni even planted a marigold in a tin can and placed it on the windowsill close to her bed. Sadly however, none of these things has helped lift her spirits.*
>
> *Frankly, we're at our wits end. We have summoned Father Manolis. Although he's been to see her several times, his visits don't*

seem to be helping either. He has blessed the house with incense and prayer, cleansing it of any evil spirits. Lately, however, he has been leaving the house with a worried look in his eyes, looking at us helplessly. Of course, Mother is unable to attend Sunday services.

Effie comes over every day to take care of her. She gets her out of bed. After walking her around the house a few times, she sits with her on the terrace for a couple of hours. She gives her sponge baths, combs her hair, and helps her change into clean clothes. As you well know, Mother and Effie have always been very close, rather more like friends than mother and daughter. Hopefully, Mother will respond soon, even if only for our sake. So far, however, we haven't seen much change in her.

Looking up at us sadly, she lets us know how much she appreciates our efforts. She reaches out to us with outstretched arms. Sometimes she just starts crying for no reason. I'm sure she wants to get better, but it seems to be out of her control at this point. We both know how important it is for Mother to feel that she is in control.

Yianni and I do the shopping and the house cleaning now, and when Effie isn't here, we do the cooking too. The land has been abandoned for the time being.

I hope that this is just a phase and that it will soon pass . . .

It hurt to read of Mother's depression. Being so far away, I felt helpless.

I remembered how I used to dance for Mother. On one occasion, Mother and I were outside on the terrace on a warm summer day. She had bought a multi-colored piece of fabric with which she intended to make a dress for me. I was very excited, having waited a long time for my special dress.

Mother started the pattern by taking my measurements. With a cloth tape measure, she carefully measured my chest from side to side, and then did the same from shoulder to waist. I then happily turned around so she could measure my back from shoulder to shoulder, then down to my waist. She then measured the length of the sleeves, and, finally, the length of the dress. All the while I stood perfectly still. She asked me the following questions: "What length do you want the dress to be? What type of collar do you want? Do you want the sleeves to have a little puff at the top where they meet at the shoulder?"

"Just below the knee and a small round collar would be fine," I responded quickly. I tried visualizing the sleeves. Finally, I announced, "I would like a small puff."

She looked at me with a smile, approving my decision. She then transferred the measurements onto an old newspaper, cutting out the dress pattern. Meanwhile, in my excitement, I wrapped the fabric around me, turning round and round. I then started to sing my favorite song, *Yerakina*. I twirled around in circles, over and over again, giggling and laughing aloud. I remember Mother egging me on, seeing how much I was enjoying myself. I danced in circles a few too many times, however, getting dizzy and falling to the ground, still laughing. Even though I felt nauseous, I got up and started to dance again. Finally, sensing that I was about to fall again, Mother pulled me to her lap. She was laughing. She kissed my hair. I felt so close to her that day. I sure loved that pretty little dress my mother made for me by hand. I wore the dress so much, it was reduced to tatters in the end. Reading my brother's letter, I wished I could be there for Mother, so I could dance for her again.

I used to read to my mother too. She loved books but having completed only third grade she could not really read. She would look at the pictures in the book to figure out the story. She especially liked fairy tales and Greek mythology. She would get a far-away look in her eyes whenever I read to her.

I would join her in this fantasy world, imagining that she was Artemis, the goddess of the hunt and the moon, running through the lush green forest bow and arrow in hand. She would chase butterflies and small animals. She would stop to drink water from a running stream. When she got tired, she would lie on the soft ground and fall asleep to the sound of the *chichigas*—grasshoppers—all around her: Heaven on Earth. I liked seeing my mother in this sublime state, so I would often ask to read to her.

I reminded myself to urge Gus to read to manoula.

If I were there, I thought, I would go to the fields and pick greens, especially dandelions, her favorite. I would bring a bunch home, and clean and cook them in boiling water. When they were cooked well, just the way she liked them, I would drain off some of the liquid, add olive oil, lemon juice and a little pepper. I would place on a cloth napkin a chunk of white bread and serve the meal to my mother in her favorite bowl, along with a small glass of red wine. I knew that she would eat it.

I believed that the depression would lift and that my mother would recover. She would be resurrected, to use her own words, like Lazarus. She just needed a little time was all, and then she would be like her old self again. I prayed for her to get better. Although it took a few months, Mother's depression finally passed.

Going Home

U ncle Tom and Auntie surprised me with a wonderful gift for my high school graduation. "How would you like to go back home and see your family?" they asked.

"What?" I stammered, for I had long ago given up any hope of returning to Greece.

"You mean, go back home?"

"Yes, just for a visit, mind you. Would you like that?" Auntie asked.

"Are you kidding? I'd love it!" I yelled, hugging them and jumping up and down.

"Now, that your uncle has finally retired," Auntie explained, "we could take a long trip to Greece. We'd leave in late March and come back in September. He hasn't been back to Greece since he left, over fifty years ago. It's about time, don't you think?"

I had no doubt that I would want nothing more than to spend spring and summer in my beloved Greece.

Since the age of sixteen, I had worked as a soda jerk after school and on weekends, at an old chocolate and soda shop called Sanders. Half of my salary went to my aunt; the other half into a savings account. I had saved almost a thousand dollars working there. Sure would help with expenses in Greece; not only might I have enough to buy everyone gifts, I reasoned, I might even be able to give my mother a little money.

I had just turned eighteen, and was about to graduate from high school.

I had applied to the University of Detroit, and if accepted, I would start in the fall. The only concern I had was leaving my high school sweetheart behind. Wayne and I had been going steady for over two years and were madly in love. We were planning on getting married once we graduated from college. A year older than me, he was completing his freshman year at Wayne State University. I knew that I would miss Wayne terribly, but we both acknowledged how much I wanted to see my family after so many years.

So, Auntie, Uncle Tom and I started making plans. Since we would be gone a long time, we bought a lot of new clothes and couple more suitcases. I bought gifts for my family: a pair of black stockings for my mother, silk stockings for my sister, neckties for my brother-in-law Nick and brother Yianni, and toys for my nieces and nephew. Placing them in suitcases, I hoped I had made the right choices.

Since Auntie was afraid of flying, we booked tickets with SS Giulio Cesare an Italian cruise line. The trip would take ten days with a stop in Naples. We would then sail to the port at Patras in northwestern Peloponnesus. From there, we would take a taxi to Skopi.

Wayne and I cried when we said goodbye. We promised to write everyday. I promised to send postcards to my girlfriends, Darlene, Sharon and Betty.

The trip to Greece was fun, immensely better than the trip to America some seven years earlier. We had good weather, and I hardly got seasick. We had first class cabins and ate all of our meals in the main dining room. During the day we swam, read, played cards and sunbathed. I wrote to Wayne most days.

Gorgeous Italian waiters would frequently come by, making sure we were not in need of anything. They would flirt with me both on deck and in the dining room. It was fun but a little nerve wrecking, too, all the attention that I was getting. I must say, I didn't quite know how to handle it. Auntie, the free spirit that she was, encouraged me to have a good time. I think she lived vicariously through me.

When we docked in Naples, Paolo, one of the waiters on ship, took me out on the town. He was intelligent, well-educated, a bit formal. He spoke English well, but was critical of Americans. He felt that, with the notable exception of America's strong economy, Americans were basically inferior to Europeans. This did not sit well with me since by this time I considered myself at least partly American. So, I refused to kiss him when our date ended.

The last day of our voyage was soon approaching. I was very excited that in less than forty-eight hours I would see my mother. She had written that she would be waiting for us in Patras.

On the morning of our scheduled arrival in Patras, I got up earlier than usual and took a quick bath. I picked out a sleeveless, light beige summer dress to wear. I hastily ate my breakfast and ran to the deck, two flights up. Lot of people were already gathered there. I could see land on the distant horizon. Greece took form as the ship slowed and approached the shore. It was a picture perfect day; clear blue skies, crystal clear waters, and a harbor filled with colorful vessels, some of which flew foreign flags. Restaurants and coffee houses were a stone's throw from shore. The cobblestone street in front of the pier was crowded with people. Seagulls rode gusts of wind overhead. The foothills glistened with little whitewashed houses. I was overcome with emotion, grateful to see my country again!

We disembarked into a crush of people going in all directions. I immediately began scanning faces, looking for that very special one that belonged to my mother. Auntie and Uncle Tom nudged me along.

"Let's find our suitcases. I'm sure we will find your mamma soon enough," Uncle Tom said.

Literally hundreds of suitcases, trunks and boxes were piled on the ground. People picked through them, looking for their belongings. As I joined in on this glorious spring's day, reminding myself that I was indeed standing on Greek soil again, I thought I heard a soft, maternal voice, "Toulaki, Toulaki."

I stood still, then slowly turned in the direction of the voice, and there she was, my manoula. Dressed as usual in black, outstretched arms beckoning me. Her eyes sparkled, but I could see that her bottom lip was quivering.

Incredibly, the sight of my mother was somehow too much to bear, so I instinctively turned away and continued looking for my suitcases. I'm not sure who got to whom first, but within seconds we were in one another's arms, hugging, kissing and sobbing. Mother then took a step back, still holding onto my hands, and looked at me from head to toe; it was as if she couldn't believe it was really me standing before her.

"You have grown up. You are so pretty. You left as a teeny-tiny little girl, and now you are s-o-o-o-o big."

Auntie and Uncle Tom stood nearby watching this mother and daughter reunion. Before I even had a chance to introduce them, Mother, with tears in her eyes, was hugging and kissing them.

"Thank you for taking such good care of Toula and bringing her back to me." I explained to Auntie what my mother had said. She understood and nodded, tears welling up in my aunt's eyes.

It took several hours to reach Skopi. We had to stop now and again because herds of sheep blocked the narrow roads. Shepherds, wielding their staffs, tried to part the woolen sea so we could pass, but sheep can be stubborn. I looked out the window at the arid, rock-strewn mountains dotted by the odd oak tree.

It was dark by the time we reached my old home. My brother Yianni was waiting for us. He was standing at the front door holding a kerosene lamp. The village was still without electricity and running water. I was reminded of Diogenes, the renowned orator of ancient Greece, searching, lantern in hand, for an honest man. Yianni had grown into a very handsome man, tall with his wavy blond hair and clear blue eyes; he looked for all the world like the actor Paul Newman. Of course, we were both overjoyed to see one another.

He had prepared some food, and encouraged us to eat. We ate a little, but we were all so exhausted that we soon went to bed. It was quite cold that first night back. All the beds were stacked with heavy, scratchy blankets that my mother and sister had woven over the years. Although they were rough to the touch, I found comfort in them in so far as they meant I was home again. I slept in the same bed—the mattress now quite worn—as I had as a little girl.

After the shock of being back home again after a long absence had worn off some, I thoroughly immersed myself in village life. Village folk came around to welcome me home. I soon became one of them again. I wanted to turn the clock back and pretend I had never left. They were curious about America and asked a million questions.

"Is it true that the streets are paved in gold?" they giggled.

I did a lot of the things that I used to do way back when. I picked fruit and wild flowers. I rode Psaris, my old horse. I got reacquainted with Hasan, my old dog and would spend hours playing fetch with him. I walked every foot of every street in town. I looked at every house, visited my old school and located my old desk. I saw some of my old schoolmates and even saw my old teacher, Mr. Paraskevopoulos. I went to the same church I had gone to so many times before. I visited my father's grave and those of others who had passed away while I was gone. I visited friends and every relative.

Mother and I went to Tripoli a number of times, and had lunch in our favorite underground restaurants. We visited bakeries, where I would have my favorite dessert, *galatobouriko,* custard pie between buttered layers of filo. We went to every festival in the area. Mother showed me off to all of her friends, relatives and even strangers whenever she had the chance.

When I was up to it, we took a little trip to Athens. We boarded a ship in Piraeus, and toured the Cyclades, a group of islands scattered across the southern Aegean Sea that includes Mykonos, Delos, Paros, and my favorite, Spetses.

We went to the ancient outdoor amphitheatre at Epidaurus, famous the world over for its phenomenal acoustics, where we saw Euripides' famous tragedy, *Medea*.

The theatre is admired for its exceptional acoustics, which permit almost perfect intelligibility of unamplified spoken words from the stage to all fourteen-thousand spectators, regardless of their seating.

A 2007 study by the Georgia Institute of Technology indicates 'that the astonishing acoustic properties may be the result of the advanced design: the rows of limestone seats filter out low-frequency sounds, such as the murmur of the crowd, and also amplify the high-frequency sounds of the stage.'

Men would follow us around, and sometimes they would even whistle. *What a pretty little American girl,* they would say. Having none of that, Mother would tell them to get lost.

I was grateful that Mother had planned so many activities for us to share, but more than anything else I wanted to go back to Skopi and bask in the simple rhythms of village life, reminiscent of my childhood. She understood. We took the bus back home, gifts and food spilling out of our colorful shopping bags.

Time flew, of course, and soon it was time for me to go back to America. I hated leaving my mother again, but it would only be a short time before we were all together again. Mother was making plans to come to America.

Epilogue

G reece was changing. Farming was fast becoming a less desirable way of making a living; it often didn't pay enough, and the work was extremely hard. So, land that had been farmed for ages, and passed from generation to generation, was now being abandoned. Instead, young people moved to the cities to find work. Office work was found by some, others worked in factories, while still others worked in tourism. More and more young people pursued higher education, enrolling in government-sponsored colleges, universities and training schools that lead to careers in such fields as medicine, law, engineering, finance, education, and civil service. Many left Greece altogether for better opportunities in America, Germany, Australia and Canada.

Mother, too, was unable to manage the land by herself, so Effie and Nick took over its daily operation. In exchange, Mother took care of their children and helped with the cooking and cleaning. They were able to rent out several parcels of land to help make ends meet. Several acres, considered valuable because of their size and proximity to both Skopi and Tripoli, were sold to families where they build their homes. Our vineyard and several other large parcels remained in the family.

Gus graduated from high school at the top of his class and left for America soon thereafter. Nick was his sponsor, and since he lived in San Francisco, Gus went there to live, too. On his way, he stopped in Detroit to spend time with me, his little sister, and to meet Auntie and Uncle Tom.

We had a wonderful time together. I gave him a tour of the Motor City, which included The Ford Automotive Manufacturing Plant, Belle Isle, Metropolitan Beach, The Great Lakes, and of course Greek town where we had dinner. I showed him my high school, Denby High, and introduced him to Wayne and my friends.

Gus wanted to become a pediatrician, and would enter medical school as soon as it was feasible financially. He was eager to get a job once he got to San Francisco.

"Any job will do; the objective for me is to save enough money as fast as I can for my college education." I had total confidence in my brilliant and intense brother.

Yianni met and married Irene, a woman ten years his senior. She lived in Tripoli with her family. After they married, they moved into their own home in Tripoli, thanks to Irene's dowry.

Effie and her husband Nick, now the proud parents of three daughters and a son, were also making plans to come to America. Nick's mother and three brothers, successful restaurateurs in Dallas, Texas, were sponsoring them. They would eventually move to San Francisco.

Uncle Tom and Auntie sold their home in Detroit, and we moved to San Francisco, too, so we could all live close to one another.

June 18, 1962, the day we had long awaited, arrived at last. My brothers and I greeted our mother upon her arrival at San Francisco International Airport. She arrived in a new land, at the age of sixty-two, full of hope and gratitude. She was finally reuniting with her children who had left her one by one some dozen years before in search of a better life in America. Yianni and his family, which now included two beautiful daughters would follow three years later.

It had taken ten years since I first left home for us all to be together again in the same city, and what a city it was, San Francisco!

49832042R00119

Made in the USA
San Bernardino, CA
06 June 2017